**MIDLOTHIAN LIBRARY SERVICE**

Please return/renew this item by the last date shown. To

D0294853

# BRILLIANT STUFF TO DO WITH DAD

## Michael Cox
### Illustrated by Clive Goddard

**■ SCHOLASTIC**

While Scholastic tries to ensure that the activities in this book are accurate, adequate or complete, it does not represent or warrant their accuracy, adequacy or completeness. All the activities contained in this book should be carried out under adult supervision. Scholastic Limited is not responsible for any accident suffered as a result of or in relation to the use of the activities contained in this book. To the extent permitted by law, Scholastic Limited excludes any liability, including any liability for negligence, for any loss and/or accident, including indirect or consequential damages arising from or in relation to the use of the activities in this book.

Scholastic Children's Books,
Euston House, 24 Eversholt Street,
London, NW1 1DB, UK

A division of Scholastic Ltd
London ~ New York ~ Toronto ~ Sydney ~ Auckland
Mexico City ~ New Delhi ~ Hong Kong

First published in the UK by Scholastic Ltd, 2012

Text copyright © Michael Cox, 2012
Illustration copyright © Clive Goddard, 2012
All rights reserved

ISBN 978 1407 12931 0

Printed and bound by CPI Group (UK) Ltd, Croydon, CR0 4YY

2 4 6 8 10 9 7 5 3

The right of Michael Cox and Clive Goddard to be identified as the author and illustrator of this work has been asserted by them in accordance with the Copyright, Designs and Patents Act, 1988.

This book is sold subject to the condition that it shall not, by way of trade or otherwise be lent, resold, hired out, or otherwise circulated without the publisher's prior consent in any form of binding or cover other than that in which it is published and without a similar condition, including this condition, being imposed on a subsequent purchaser.

# CONTENTS

# INTRODUCTION

Nowadays many boys and girls don't get to spend as much time with their dads as they did in times gone by. In the past, they'd stand shoulder-to-shoulder with him as he did battle with sabre-toothed tigers, or scare off crows as he tended fields full of carrots, hanging on his every word as he taught them the art of cobbling, carpentry, bricklaying, fish gutting, (picking pockets, robbing stagecoaches), or whatever trade the family had been in for generations.

And in that way these boys and girls would share all sorts of challenging, exciting and satisfying experiences

5

with their dad (whilst receiving regular smacks round the ear-hole). And, quite naturally, in the process, they'd get to know each other so much better.

However, in this modern age of non-stop hustle and bustle, information overload and biodegradable bottom-wipes, many dads, and mums, for that matter, are busy working all hours. And when dads come home, exhausted from spending 16 hours shampooing poodles, selling dreams, mending broken hearts, shouting at people, or whatever other job they do, they simply flake out in front of the telly, leaving many children wondering who that strange man on the settee is.

So, with the idea of getting you and your dad to get to know each other better, or to simply enrich your already fantastic relationship, here are some brilliant activities to share with him. They range from simple, fun activities such as learning to whip a tablecloth from under a load of plates without breaking them and making a zombie's face you can eat, to more challenging projects like growing a little 'garden of horrors', designing and building your own miniature golf course and breeding tarantulas for pleasure and profit.

So what are you waiting for? Take your dad by the scruff of his neck, drag him away from the TV and get sharing these brilliant activities.

---

## HEALTH AND SAFETY WARNING! ⊖⊖

Several of these activities are dangerous! Some of them involve extremely hazardous things like knives, fire, flesh-eating plants and marzipan. So please take care! The publishers of this book can in no way accept responsibility if, as a result of carrying out these activities, your dad ends up super-glued to a railway line, crushed by a giant pumpkin, or is sent to prison for scaring an old-age pensioner shirtless. Also, please be aware that while you and your dad are enjoying any of these activities there is a million to one chance that you will be struck by lightning, bitten by a pit-bull Chihuahua or ripped to shreds by rabid, 10-foot-tall cannibals who have decided to invade Planet Earth on the day you choose to build a bridge across a stream. So, please ... be prepared!

# PUT A GHOST IN YOUR GARDEN

Make a really scary chicken-wire ghostly apparition and scare the living daylights out of your visitors. Chicken wire is thin wire woven into hexagon shapes and it's usually used to stop chickens crossing the road or being eaten by foxes – that sort of thing. However, because it's so very strong and flexible, it's also brilliant for making 3D shapes, including this extremely scary looking phantom.

## WHAT YOU NEED ↓

- 3 metres of 25-mm diameter chicken wire
- Some wire cutters or tin snips
- Work gloves to protect your hands
- Wire ties (Not absolutely necessary,
You can use bits of chicken wire instead)
- Safety goggles
- Flat-nose pliers
- Imagination

## WHAT TO DO

**1** Unroll your chicken wire. Just like a terrified hedgehog, the pesky stuff will immediately try to roll itself back up again because it's so incredibly springy (and terrified). To stop this happening, once you've got it flat, weigh it down with something really heavy (such as a sumo wrestler ... or Derbyshire). Now leave it a while to allow it to get used to the idea of being completely non-cylindrical.

**2** Once your chicken wire is totally resigned to the idea of being flat you can roll it up again! Not into a tight tube, but into a cylinder that more or less matches the dimensions of your intended ghost. However, before you do this, you might want to trim your wire with your tin snips. It all depends on the size of the ghost you're planning to create.

**3** To do this, carefully snip through each hexagon shape until your section of wire can be separated from the rest.

**4** Secure the edges of your chicken-wire cylinder with wire ties, being careful not to let them scratch you or poke you in the eye (or eyes, if you've two of them).

**5** Now for the creative fun bit. By gently kneading, sculpting, snipping, folding and teasing the chicken-wire cylinder, you can begin to shape your ghost.

**6** For a simple ghost you probably won't need to create separate body parts, but if you want to make a more elaborate ghost such as one carrying its own severed head, waving its arms around, trying to climb back into its own grave (or scratching its bottom), you'll have to knock up some extra bits.

**7** To do this, cut sections of wire into the sizes you need, then sculpt the extra bits for your ghost before finally attaching them to the main figure with wire ties or off-cuts of chicken wire.

**8** Now site your phantom in a place where it is guaranteed to cause maximum terror, for example, in the woods just near that Scout and Guide camp on a misty morning ... ooer! However, remember that when 'embedding' your ghost it's got to be far enough away from your intended victims for them not to realize it's chicken wire or they'll just think it's a designer hen coop.

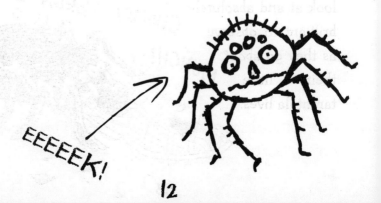

EEEEEK!

# KEEP PET TARANTULAS

Keeping pet tarantulas is a challenging and fascinating thing to do. It's also something you could even turn into a little business, selling your hairy little babies to friends and family. But before you tackle that mega-exciting challenge, you must first get to grips with the basics of tarantula keeping, which are, in themselves, challenging, fun, exciting and extremely rewarding.

WHY KEEP PET TARANTULAS? Tarantulas make good pets because, unlike parrots and Yorkshire Terriers, they're very, very quiet (especially when they're sleeping). Also, unlike Great Danes, ponies and baby elephants, they require very little space. And of course, they're great to look at and absolutely brilliant to observe as they go about their little tarantula lives.

CHOMP!

GRONFF!

MUNCH!

13

CHOOSING YOUR TARANTULA. There are about 800 different sorts of tarantulas in the world. But, unless you're the sort of person who has to 'tick all the boxes', you don't actually have to keep and breed all 800 species. One of the most popular tarantulas for keeping as a pet is the Brazilian Black as it's quite docile, but very impressive looking (and, with patience, can be taught to sit up and beg and fetch slippers). However, the one to really avoid is the King Baboon, which comes from Africa (and would rip off your leg as soon as look at you).

HOUSING. Tarantulas are not all that fussed about what sort of house you keep them in, be it humble terrace, country cottage or mansion, but once you've got them in your house be sure to provide them with a 'terrarium' in which to spend their days in peace. The best thing for this is a fish tank with a top, which you should keep in a warm area of your house or heat to a temperature of 70–80°F with a small, specially designed electric pad (or a furry hot water bottle, which the tarantula will think is its mum).

Spread a layer of sterilized potting compost over its bottom (the tank's bottom not the tarantula's) and make sure you put in a dish of drinking water and a little hidey-hole made from sticks and little rocks. You might also like to decorate your tarantula's new abode with a few snapshots of Rio de Janeiro and the Brazilian rainforest to stop it feeling homesick.

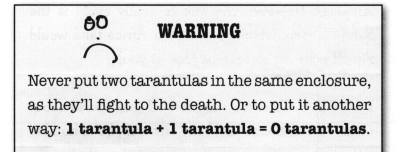

**WARNING**

Never put two tarantulas in the same enclosure, as they'll fight to the death. Or to put it another way: **1 tarantula + 1 tarantula = 0 tarantulas**.

HANDLING YOUR TARANTULAS. Take care when handling your tarantulas and do it as little as possible, if at all. If you do have to pick them up, hold them securely between the second and third pair of legs with your thumb and forefinger. Also be aware that they're as fast as lightning and, if dropped, will be up your Aunty Hilda's trouser leg in a flash.

15

FEEDING. While keeping your pet spider, feel free to eat what ever you like: chips, cream eggs, bananas or whatever, but you must feed your tarantulas on a more specialized diet. In the wild, tarantulas mainly eat insects and other spiders but the bigger ones also prey on lizards, mice, birds (and little old ladies). The best things to feed captive tarantulas are the chirpy insects known as crickets.

MOLTING. If you see your tarantula laying on its back in its cage it's either a) dead or b) molting. Molting is the process where it sheds its skin and hairs because its growing body has become too big for them. It usually takes between 15 minutes and several hours.

### NB Don't disturb it while this is happening or it may well die!

HOW TO DEAL WITH AN ENRAGED PET TARANTULA: If your tarantula is annoyed with you it will first begin to hurl hairs at you in order to cause you painful, but temporary, skin irritation in the form of a rash. But if it's really miffed it will rear up on its back legs and reveal its fangs as a prelude to sinking its gnashers into your flesh. The best thing to do if this happens is to a) Run away. b) Use your dad as a 'human shield'. But seriously, if you do happen to get nipped by little 'Boris' just dab the bite with some antiseptic and you'll soon get over it. However, if you are allergic to bee stings and suchlike, you must get medical help immediately.

# MAKE A DINOSAUR OUT OF
# BENDY BALLOONS

## WHAT YOU NEED ↘

• Modelling balloons: you can buy packs of these from a party shop or on the Internet By far the safest, easiest and quickest way to blow them up is with a professional pump that has a 'nibbed' end.

• Unlimited imagination. You'll be amazed at the variety of bizarre bendy balloon creations you can come up with once you put your mind to it — anything from simple cats and hats to dinosaurs and three-headed space monsters.

• Permanent markers to add faces, patterns, pictures or writing to your balloon creations.

GRRRRR! →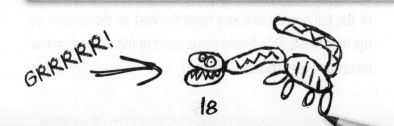

**WHAT TO DO**

Practice; get the 'feel' of balloon bending using just one balloon.

**1** Blow up a balloon using a balloon pump.

**NB: Resist the temptation to make rude noises by stretching your balloon and slowly letting the air out of it. It's not funny and it's not clever! HA!**

Well, all right, it is quite funny.

**2** Don't inflate the entire balloon. Leave a few inches at the end for the air to go into when you start twisting.

**3** Loop the end of the balloon around two of your fingers and tie a knot in it to stop the air escaping.

**4** Practice a 'fold twist' and 'locking off'. To do this, make two bubbles about as long as your finger then bring the rest of the balloon around and twist the rest of the balloon on the first twist. This technique is used to make most animal heads and legs. Now you're ready to…

# MAKE A **DINOSAUR**

**WHAT YOU NEED** ↓
Two standard modelling balloons

**WHAT YOU DO** ↘

Make two bubbles about as long as your finger, then fold, bring the knot around and twist it onto the second twist. It doesn't matter how you twist the knot so long as it doesn't come undone. This is your dinosaur's head and jaws.

Now it's time to make the dinosaur's neck, front legs and body from the rest of the balloon. Make another longer bubble for the neck, twist, make two more bubbles for the legs, bring them round and twist to

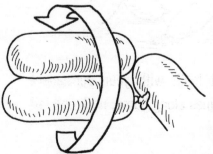

lock off. You should now have the head, neck, two front legs and body.

Take your second balloon. Make three bubbles the same length as the two front legs for the back legs and tail. Bend round and lock off as before.

Attach the back legs and tail to the end of the body (which should have a handy little bit of un-inflated balloon). The fourth, longer bubble is the humped back. Curve this over the other bit of the dinosaur body and twist the end bit between the neck and legs so that it doesn't come undone.

Add eyes, nostrils and teeth with your permanent markers, and draw zigzag lines along hump, neck and tail for the back spines.

# CHANGE A CAR WHEEL

Believe it or not, quite soon you will be old enough to take your driving test. Then, once you've passed it, you'll be tootling around in the family car or, if you're lucky, your own car. But, having passed your test, will you be prepared for one of the most annoying, frustrating, and possibly dangerous, things that might happen to you when you're driving: getting a flat tyre? And even worse than that, getting a flat tyre on a freezing cold, dark, rainy night on a lonely country lane or motorway hard shoulder? So why not be prepared for those pesky punctures that happen to all motorists at some time or other? Get your dad to show you how to change a car wheel.

## WHAT YOU NEED ↘
• The family car and the car's spare wheel and tyre, which should be properly inflated.
• The car's jack. This is the handy gadget that enables you to lift the car off the ground so that you can change the wheel (and you thought you were a such a wimp!).

- The car's handbook which shows you where to attach the jack to the car.
- A brace or a wheel-nut wrench with extension bar. This is to remove the nuts which hold the wheel on.
- A locking wheel-nut adaptor if your car is fitted with anti-theft wheel nuts*. (*Usually fitted when the wheels are worth more than the actual car.)
- At least one wheel chock. That's a wedge-shaped thing to stop the car rolling.

- A screwdriver
- Gloves: the wheel and tyre will be filthy (and so would you be if you'd spent your entire life rolling around on the ground).
- Something to kneel on.
- A torch, just in case it gets dark while you're still wheel changing (plus survival rations if it takes even longer than that).
- A reflective jacket and strong, sensible shoes.

## WHAT TO DO

**1** Choose a dry warm day for changing the wheel at home.

**2** Get your dad to park the car on firm ground – never change a wheel on soft or unstable ground.

**3** Look at the car handbook to find out where the 'jacking points' are.

**4** Make sure the car engine's not running and switch on the hazard warning lights.

**5** Put on the handbrake and put the car in first gear – your dad will show you how to do this.

**6** 'Chock' the wheel diagonally across from the one you're changing.

**7** Take the spare wheel from the car boot and lay it on the ground in a handy spot.

**8** Remove the wheel trim if there is one. You may have to lever it off with a screwdriver.

**9** Position the jack at the handbook-recommended lifting point closest to the wheel you're changing.

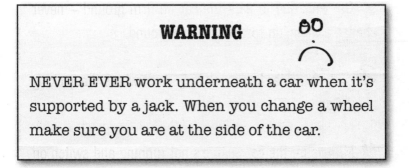

## WARNING

NEVER EVER work underneath a car when it's supported by a jack. When you change a wheel make sure you are at the side of the car.

**10** Make sure the jack 'head' slots neatly into the jacking point as shown in the handbook then start to open the jack until it just begins to lift the car on its 'springs'. You usually do this by turning a handle on the jack.

**11** Use your car's wheel brace – and wheel-nut adapter if necessary – to slacken off the wheel nuts or bolts.

**12** Use the jack to lift the car a bit more so that its wheel is just clear of the ground.

**13** Leaving the top one until last, use the brace or wrench to remove the wheel nuts or bolts while keeping the wheel on its hub by pressing it with your knee. The wheel will want to swing around as you take off the nuts.

**14** Take off the last nut or bolt and lift the wheel away from the hub.

**15** Position the spare wheel on the hub then replace the bolts or nuts. Fit the top one first and only tighten them with your fingers.

**16** Using the jack, carefully lower the wheel until it's on the ground.

**17** Now use the brace or wrench to tighten up the bolts or nuts as far as they will go.

**18** Remove the jack from the jacking point.
You're finished! Well done, you completed a task that quite a lot of adults have difficulty doing and are you now prepared for the inevitable 'flat'.

## WARNING

If you ever do get a flat tyre NEVER try to change it at the side of the road or on a motorway 'hard shoulder'. Pull into safe spot away from traffic or ring for help. Most motorway accidents involve people with flat tyres or broken-down cars being killed or injured on the 'hard shoulder'!

# MAKE A BRIDGE BETWEEN TWO FISH TANKS AND WATCH YOUR PET FISH OR TADPOLES SWIM ACROSS IT

This is a fun and exciting project that's based on simple physics (and even simpler water creatures). Once you've set up your bridge and your little aquatic dimwits have got the idea of using it to travel from one tank to the other it will give you, and them, hours of endless fun. It really does look like your tadpoles or fish are 'flying' between the two tanks.

## HOW IT WORKS

It's all based on physics, hydraulics, science gubbins and whatnot (to put it technically). Try raising an inverted bottle of water out of a bucket of water and you'll see that the water will remain in the bottle as long as no air is allowed to enter it. The principle is the same as that on which a hamster water bottle works, with the level of water in the drinking bowl always remaining constant. This is because water is heavier than air (and – not many people know this – hamsters are very scary little paranormal beings who are able to the control the natural elements simply by 'willing' them to act in a certain way).

**WHAT YOU NEED**

- Two fish tanks
- Some fish or tadpoles
- A glass tube – or some straight clear plastic tube and two of those little plastic 'elbows' that plumbers use to make pipes turn corners. If you're using glass tube you'll also need a Bunsen burner and heat-proof gloves.

**Important:** Make sure the diameter of your tube is wide enough to allow your fish and tadpoles to swim through (as you don't want the really fat ones getting stuck).

## WHAT TO DO

*1* Your main aim is to create a tube with two bends that will allow you two suspend one end below the water's surface in one aquarium and the other end below the water's surface in the other aquarium.

*2* If you're using glass tube, rather than plastic, you'll definitely need your dad to do the tricky bits. Wearing the heatproof gloves he must hold the part of the glass tube you need to bend over the flame of the bunsen burner.

**NB To spread the heat it's best to attach a device called a fish-tail to the burner.**

When this section's soft, holding the cold parts of the glass, he must make the 45-degree bend which will rest on the top of one of the tanks. Now repeat the process for the other bend.

**3** If you're using plastic tubes use the 'elbows' to create the bends.

**4** Now fill your 'bridge' with water, preferably rainwater or water that's been allowed to stand for 48 hours so that the chlorine can escape.

**5** Keeping a thumb over each open end of the bridge turn it over and lower the ends into the two tanks, making sure no air enters them.

**NB If you want to go all fancy-pants with this project you can make little support brackets to keep the tube stable. Failing that a bit of Blu-tak or a couple of double-sided sticky wotsits will do.**

COR, WHAT FUN!

# A TOWERING ACHIEVEMENT

## LEARN TO WALK ON STILTS

Want to go up in the world? Then why not learn to walk on stilts. Stilts have been around for thousands of years. Sometimes they're used for fun and, at other times, for work. For instance, in parts of France, shepherds use them to cross marshy places while guarding their flocks. They're great fun to walk on (stilts, not shepherds) and give you an entirely new perspective on the world around you. There are lots of different sorts of stilts: simple hand-held ones; ones you strap to your legs, leaving your hands free to wave, or to pat the 'bone-domes' of passing bald men; hinged ones; tripod-shaped ones which plasterers use when they're working on high walls or ceilings; and bendy stilts that allow you to sort of 'stilt bounce' rather than stilt walk. As a beginner, it's best to use the simple hand-held stilts that our activity involves. You can buy them, or you and your dad can make them quite cheaply.

Take this altitude aptitude test: check your suitability for stilt walking by trying to walk on your heels. If you can do that, you're probably going to be able to 'walk tall'. However, if you're the sort of person who can't walk without tripping over an ant or gets dizzy just walking upstairs, you probably aren't cut out for stilt walking.

Safety: Stilt walking is exciting and loads of fun but also quite dangerous. Always wear skateboarder's knee, wrist and elbow pads and a crash helmet. That way, if you do crash to the ground, you'll be protected. However, when you are stilt walking, remember the golden rule of the professional stilt walker:

NEVER FALL!

## HERE'S HOW TO STILT WALK…

**1** First, get onto your stilts. You can either a) put your back against a wall, leaning your stilts against it, then climb onto them using the wall for support or b) get your dad to hold the stilts still while you climb onto them, again 'backing' onto them or c) also with the help of your dad, sit on the roof of the family car and ease yourself onto them (but preferably not when it's being driven to the shops).

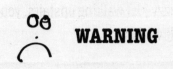

## WARNING

Whatever you do, don't try to hold your stilts in front of you then climb onto them, as you'll be sure to overbalance – this is a common beginners' mistake (also a posh beginners' mistake).

**2** Take your first steps safely. The best way to do this is to tightly tie a rope between a couple of trees, poles or lampposts, so that it's at a level midway between your waist and your armpit when you're up on your stilts. Or you could use a tightly tied washing line (preferably without any washing on it). That way, if you do lose your balance you, can quickly grab the rope for support.

**3** Now walk on the spot, alternately lifting your legs, so that your stilt is about 15 cm off the ground. As you do, be aware that you're shifting your weight from one leg to the other. With practice, you will get used to the weight of the stilts and feel that you are beginning to 'control' them.

**4** You're ready to try taking your first steps. This is rather like the 'lifting-the-feet' bit you've just done but you'll now be placing your feet a little further forward each time you lift. In other words you are now stilt walking (or lying in a pathetically mangled and pitifully sobbing heap on the ground).

**5** Now it's time to carefully work your way along the rope with your dad walking alongside you, just in case you loose your balance.

**6** Having reached the end of the rope, you face your next big challenge: turning around! To do this, 'pivot' on one foot, whilst lifting the other. At this point your dad must be extra vigilant (e.g. not reading a book or chatting with a neighbour).

**7** Now walk back along the rope. Repeat the 'rope-walking' until you gain a real sense of confidence and control over your stilts (and your dad).

**8** As a someone learning to ride a bike might say, 'It's now time to throw away the stabilizers', or in the case of stilt walking, leave the rope behind. To do this get your dad to back away from the rope then walk towards him, making sure he's always near enough to catch you if you fall.

**9** If you practice this routine every day for a week or so, you will gain in confidence. One really important thing to remember: stilt walking is very tiring. However, if you stop for a breather, you'll most definitely fall over! Only really accomplished stilt walkers are able to stand completely still on their stilts. So remember to pace yourself.

**10** A word about falling. If you do find yourself losing your balance make sure that you don't fall backwards, or sideways, because you'll really hurt yourself. Instead, try your best to fall forwards, whilst leaning back slightly so that your footrests absorb the impact of the fall. Next, let your knees take the impact. Those knee pads should come in really useful now. And, at this point, your rate of fall will have slowed considerably so it probably won't hurt when you finally hit the ground. But one really important thing to remember when you're falling is NOT to put out your hands to break your fall or you'll end up with broken wrists.

OOOOOOPS!

# CREATE A HUGE, HUGE DRAMA WITH A DIORAMA

Imagine you're an all-powerful super-being with the ability to travel through time and space, in reality and fantasy. You will be able to spy on the Battle of Hastings, watch Neanderthals stampeding mammoths over cliffs or peep into the weird world of Alice in Wonderland. Where you are standing is the 'here and now', but what you are peering at is somewhere very different and quite magical — a scene that will set your imagination racing. That's the effect that the three-dimensional miniature worlds known as 'dioramas' have on many people.

For loads of reasons, making your very own diorama is brilliant fun! You use your artistic and creative skills to the full. You learn tons of stuff as you research the details of the setting. You stretch your imagination to its limits. You also pick up lots of new skills as you handle all the different materials involved. And finally, you end up with a miniature world which will not only impress your friends but is also a place where you can tell stories, play games and act out all sorts of scintillating scenarios.

**WHAT TO DO**

**1** Choose your theme. The setting for your diorama is limited only by your imagination. It could be a scene from a sci-fi movie where giant cockroaches bite the heads off terrified humans, or a fairytale castle and village where handsome knights woo pretty maidens, horses drink from the duck pond and happy peasants bring in the harvest (or, if you're that way inclined, unhappy peasants suffer agonizing deaths from the bubonic plague). It could be your take on what a city of the future might look like or what your own city, town or village may have looked like 300 years ago. It could be a spooky churchyard filled with zombies, skeletons and vampires complete with special effects like swirling mist and hooting owls. Or it could be the scene of a disaster such as the Great Fire of London or the destruction of Pompeii by the erupting Mount Vesuvius. You could even make dioramas based on famous paintings. The possibilities are endless!

**2** Get inspired by other people's dioramas. Science and natural history museums have some of the best dioramas in the world. They should be, they're made by professionals. Stuffed animals in glass cases are also set in imaginative dioramas. Another place to check out some really awesome dioramas is to Google images on the Internet, for instance those by a chap called Paul Smith, which look totally real!

**3** Research the historical and visual details of your diorama using the Internet and libraries. Then let your imagination run wild as you sketch out a plan for your 3D diorama drama.

**4** Choose a scale for your diorama. For instance, one seventy-fifth of actual size or a twentieth of actual size. Stick to the scale to make your diorama look realistic.

**5** Get your tools together.

- A ruler
- Scissors
- A craft knife
- A pencil
- A hack-saw
- A file
- Paint brushes
- Paint
- Glue
- Tweezers
- Needle-nose pliers
- A small vice

This last item will be really useful for holding small fiddly bits of your diorama as you glue or paint them.

TIP: ACRYLIC PAINT IS BEST FOR DIORAMAS - IT'S WATER-BASED AND QUICK DRYING.

**6** Choose a base for your scene. This could be a piece of wood, foam board or polystyrene, or even an old shoebox if you want to begin with a very small-scale diorama. Decide whether your base will have back and side walls where you'll create 'background' scenery like that which you see in theatres and old movies.

**7** Get your materials together. These will include...

- Modelling clay
- Plaster of Paris
- Old newspapers
- Plaster-of-Paris-coated bandage
- Cardboard cut from cereal boxes
- Masking tape

42

- Filler
- Balsa wood
- Varnish
- Kitchen towel
- Putty
- Twigs
- Stones
- Sawdust
- Grass
- Dried herbs
- Kitchen foil

Be imaginative and ingenious in your choice of 'props'. You'll be amazed what you find just by looking around your garden.

**8** Rough out the 'terrain' for your diorama. This could be hilly, mountainous or, easiest of all, completely flat, for instance, if you're creating a Dutch windmill scene. If you want to make hills, one way to do it is to scrunch up newspaper then lay strips of card over it held in place by masking tape. Once you've got your hills cover them in plaster of Paris bandage, papier-mâché or quick-drying modelling clay. And if you're making a seascape diorama use your modelling clay to make waves and ripples.

**9** Paint your terrain and give it texture. This is where you'll be employing your creative talents and imagination. And don't forget to experiment with different materials to create the effects you're after.

**10** Start to add the features of your diorama. Of course, what they are will depend on the theme you've chosen. Things you'll be adding might include trees, people, buildings, vehicles and animals. Always start adding the features from the back part of your diorama in order to avoid damaging what you've already put in place. And don't forget that, as well as painting objects, you can use your digital camera and your computer printer to create realistic looking 'facades' for buildings and backdrops.

**11** Now's the time to add those all-important details to your scene that you discovered when you were doing your background research.

**12** As you become more skilled and knowledgeable you might like to bring your diorama to life with some 'special effects'. This is where your dad could get involved big-time, especially if he's a whizz with computers or electronics.

## THINGS YOU MIGHT CONSIDER INCLUDE:

a) Smoke or mist effects created using a model-railway enthusiasts' smoke-generator.

b) Sound effects such as screams, thunder, howling wolves, bird song or rushing water. You can download some of these from your computer then play them through an ipod dock.

c) Water effects.

d) Use lights to create a spooky glow from windows, flashes from an erupting volcano or the flicker of a distant bonfire.

e) Using mirrors to make part of your diorama to look loads bigger than it is.

f) Working parts like drawbridges, trebuchets and guillotines.

Have fun! You never know, you may be laying the foundations for a career in movie set-making and special effects.

# GET IN TOUCH WITH YOUR INNER NEANDERTHAL

## GO CAMPING IN THE WILD WITHOUT A TENT

At one time, every human being in the world went camping in the wild without a tent. Mainly because tents hadn't been invented and the entire world was very, very wild! By wandering off into a really wild place and surviving wind, rain, hunger, freezing cold, scorching sun, attacks from wild animals and more, you and your dad will have your courage and resourcefulness tested to their limits, finally discovering that you are either...

a) A tough team/dynamic duo of resourceful, brave and cunning 'die-hards' who are unfazed by bears, boa constrictors or blizzards and who thrive on all sorts of tricky and challenging situations, the more dangerous the better!

b) A pair of complete wimps whose idea of a having a really hard time is sitting on the settee drinking cocoa and watching the Antiques Road Show.

## WHAT TO DO

Go to a really wild place such as the Scottish Highlands, the Brecon Beacons in Wales, the Himalayas, the Brazilian rainforest (or Nottingham) equipped with basic food and survival gear. This should include:

- A head torch
- First-aid kit
- A knife
- Loo roll
- A map
- A compass
- Matches in a waterproof container
- Candles
- Water
- Water purification tablets
- High-energy food
- Gold or silver emergency foil blankets (and a top-quality helicopter)

Also make sure you're suitably dressed for the conditions you'll encounter.

Once you're out in the wilderness you'll soon begin to enjoy the feeling of freedom and excitement as your primitive self, which has been buried just below the surface for hundreds of generations, starts to emerge. In no time you'll tune in to nature and be aware of squirrels, rabbits, birds, subtle changes in the weather and terrain. You may even begin to feel like a wild animal yourself!

GRR, SNARL, GNASH!

Of course, after a day's trekking, your number-one priority will be to find somewhere safe, warm and dry to spend the night. Handy places to spend the night, without actually having to build a shelter, include caves, underneath the branches of fallen trees, large rocks, bushes, cosy holes and crevices (and Premier Travel Inns). However, if there are none of these handy, you will have to build your own survival shelter (see page 69).

# MAKE A DELICIOUS MEDITERRANEAN FISH STEW

Even on the darkest, coldest winter days, one mouthful, or even just a whiff of this delicious dish will transport you and your guests to the sunlit shores of the clear blue Mediterranean Sea. It's easy to make, and when they taste it your family and friends will marvel at your culinary skills. And cooking up this wonderful meal may be your first step on the road to super-chef stardom!

## WHAT YOU NEED

SERVES 2

• Jar of anchovies in oil – only use 1 or 2 though
• Good slosh of extra virgin olive oil
• 4 garlic cloves, crushed
• Glass of red wine
• Tin of chopped tomatoes
• Couple of dollops of sun-dried tomato paste
• Pinch of chilli, or a few drops of Tabasco sauce
• Dusting of black pepper

- Fist full of well-chopped fresh parsley
- 2 medium-sized old potatoes or 5 new ones – peeled and cut to into 2-cm cubes
- 3 defrosted white-fish blocks or cod or coley (filleted)
- Whole red pepper (capsicum) – pith and seeds removed and sliced
- Bag of prepared squid (from a supermarket fish counter)
- Pack of cooked or uncooked king prawns

**NB – don't use salt in the recipe, as the anchovies are really salty**

**WHAT TO DO**

Heat the olive oil and add the crushed garlic, chilli, black pepper, the chopped parsley and one or two anchovies.

Stir continuously on a medium heat to form the stew base – the anchovies should sort of 'melt' into the mixture.

Add the spuds and stir until they begin to go golden, sloshing in a bit of the wine and juice from the tinned tomatoes if the mixture begins to look too dry

Chop the squid into little rings then add them and their tentacles to the mixture – stir for a minute or three.

Add the rest of the tomatoes, the tomato puree, the diced red pepper and the wine and bring to the boil, stirring continuously.

GLOP!

BLOOP!

PLOP!

Turn the heat down, cover with a lid and let the mixture simmer for 20 minutes.

Break up the white fish, add to the mixture and let it simmer another 25 minutes, stirring every now and again.

Add the prawns two or three minutes before serving and bring the mixture to the boil.

Serve with crusty French bread.

Some people serve this with garlic mayonnaise sauce – however, it does make it very rich. There are tons of variations of the Mediterranean fish-stew recipe on the Internet but some of them are quite involved and labour intensive. You can prepare this version quite quickly and easily and it still tastes great.

BON APPETIT!

# PLAY TIN CAN LURKY

'Tin can lurky', or 'kick the can', as boring people call it, is a hiding and seeking game involving skill, strategy, stealth, nimbleness, niftiness and a lot of undignified shouting. It's also tons of fun!

## WHAT YOU NEED ↓

• About a dozen people to play the game, but if you're short, it can be played with a minimum of three.

WHO ARE YOU CALLING A MINI MUM OF THREE?

AND WHO ARE YOU CALLING SHORT?

## IMPORTANT EDUCATIONAL NOTE:

All of the players should be able to count to at least 100. However, if someone is unable to

ONE, TWO, FIVE, THREE...

count to 100 they may recite a poem (or chant the entire Telephone Directory) instead.

• **A TIN CAN:** which doesn't need to be able to count at all

A TIN CAN

PEAS*

\* PEAS ARE OPTIONAL

• **AN OUTDOOR SPACE** with lots of hiding places e.g. a park, local woods, waste ground, Wales, the Amazon...

There are loads of variations of the game but to avoid causing confusion for readers who are slightly hard-of-thinking this is the version which was traditionally played by children in the 1950s who were forced to keep at it all day long simply to keep from dying of hypothermia due to the fact that in those days they didn't have central heating, warm clothes, over-protective parents or nourishing meals.

## HEALTH AND SAFETY WARNING

Tin-can-lurky players can become very over-excited and get so carried away by all the running, hiding and shouting that they become completely oblivious to all manner of imminent dangers, so it's a good idea to avoid playing the game in the vicinity of cliffs, busy motorways, prisoner-of-war camps, exposed mine shafts and safari parks.

**WHAT TO DO**

**1** Someone is chosen to be 'on'. You could simply put it to a vote, craftily choosing someone who is totally rubbish at running and whose observational skills are non-existent, thus ensuring they remain 'on' for ever. However, more fairly, it would be reasonable to draw straws or do that ridiculous stone, paper, scissors twaddle to decide who is going to be 'on'.

**2** The 'on' person stands in an open space, known as 'home' which is, ideally, a little hill surrounded by lots of bushes, caves, trees, humps, hollows, etc, where the 'off' people can hide out. This open space also doubles as a jail where 'prisoners' will be held.

**3** 'On' covers their eyes with their hands and counts to 100. While they're counting everyone else goes and hides (or goes home). Alternatively, one of the 'off' bods who is really good at kicking, boots the can with all their might and while 'on' is retrieving it then returning to the space, every one similarly goes and hides. At the end of counting or can-retrieving the 'on' yells, "Coming ready or not!"

**4** 'On' tries to find the hiders. They can do this by simply scanning the terrain for exposed legs, ears, noses etc, listening out for chuckles, twigs breaking, involuntarily and humiliating escapes of intestinal gases – that sort of thing – or they can go hunting for the hiders. However, packs of bloodhounds, Sioux Indian trackers and helicopters with heat-seeking thermal-imaging devices are not permitted during this part of the game.

**5** When 'on' discovers an 'off' they must yell their name* and tag them then race back to the can and place their foot on it, thus rendering the hider 'captured'. However if the 'tagged' person is able to reach the can and kick it first, the 'on' must retrieve it and return it to the spot, and is without capturing power until they have done so, by which time the prisoner should have escaped and once more hidden themselves. This can be rather a frustrating moment for the 'on' person, especially if it happens 20 or 30 times, at which point they may be tempted to go home and play with their Etch-a-Sketch or watch The Lone Ranger.

**\* For this reason, it's not a good idea to play the game with complete strangers.**

**6** If the prisoner does not manage to escape like this and is now effectively in jail, it's the task of the other hiders to rescue them. The opportunity to do this arises when 'on' is busy searching for other hiders and the 'would-be' rescuer stealthily, crawls, wriggles, abseils, tunnels, teleports their way to the can, undetected by the 'on' and gives it an almighty kick, thus freeing the prisoner. If there are several prisoners, the one who was caught first is the one to be freed. Or, to put it another way, mass breakouts are not permitted.

**7** The game ends when either:

a) 'On' catches all of the players, at which point the person who has been held prisoner longest, or the one who was caught first, becomes the new 'on' (or is paroled for good behaviour).

b) Everyone collapses with dehydration and heat exhaustion and is rushed to hospital.

c) The local truant officer takes everyone back to school

d) A dog steals the can.

# OPTIONAL EXTRAS

a) During the game all players are welcome to yell, "Olly, olly, oxen free!" or "All ye, all ye, out and free" at any time. No one is quite sure what these traditional and rather embarrassing tin-can-lurky calls mean exactly, but they certainly give the game the magical and mysterious sense that it may well have been played since the dawn of time, which is, of course, nonsense, because tin cans were only invented in the 1800s.

b) Another very entertaining version of the game, which really does call on the stealth skills of the hiders, involves the 'on' covering their eyes and counting to 30 at intervals throughout the game. During these counts it's the task of the hiders to make their way back to the hill, finding suitable hiding places on the way, eventually reaching 'home' whilst the 'on' has their eyes covered and thus making themselves 'safe'.

c) Of course, what has been described above refers to British tin can lurky but there are many more versions all over the world including Kenyan Masaai 'big gourd lurky' which takes in long-distance running, spears and lions and Dutch 'big rubbery cheese lurky' involving canal-swimming and windmill-leaping.

**INTERESTING FACT:** It's rumoured that some ancient and extremely competitive 1950s tin-can-lurky players, determined to remain undetected in their perfect hiding places, remain in them to this day, totally unaware that their game actually finished several decades ago, their playmates having wandered off and got on with the grown-up business of getting jobs, getting married and having children and grandchildren.

IT'S ALL RIGHT, BERT. YOU CAN COME OUT NOW!

ALL RIGHT. BUT ONLY IF YOU SAY I'M THE WINNER

# GO BEACH COMBING

## THERE ARE TWO WAYS TO DO THIS:

a) Go to a cliff top on a dark and stormy winter's night and lure a passing sailing ship, preferably laden with luxury goods, to its doom by waving a lantern to give the captain the impression he is nearing a 'safe haven'. Once the ship has been dashed to pieces on the rocks below and its cargo has been washed ashore, help yourself to the goodies. NB. This method, though very profitable, may well result in you and your dad being hung by the neck until you are dead, or spending the rest of your life in prison, if you happen to get caught by the authorities. Therefore, you'd probably be much better to go for the next method:

b) The best time to do beach combing that doesn't involve shipwrecks, drowned 'jack-tars' and court appearances is also winter because that is the time when storms and high tides stir objects from the depths of the ocean and sweep them ashore. That said, all seasons have their own sort of treasures.

Due to things like magnetism, the moon (and the ever-present, all-powerful Sea Gods), on most beaches the tide comes in twice a day. Every time it does, it leaves a fresh hoard of treasure, along

with a few things you definitely don't want anything to do with, including blobs of oil, used toilet tissue (and the severed ears of long-dead pirates).

## WHAT TO DO

Walk along the strandline, or high-water mark as it's also known, searching for odd-looking piles of sand and knots of seaweed that may well be concealing something absolutely amazing. There's a good chance you'll come across shells, seahorses that have galloped their last gallop, dead seabirds, starfish, dead seals, animal skeletons, jellyfish, shark egg cases or messages in bottles. Or, just as interestingly, it could be pieces of driftwood which have been eroded into astonishing shapes by the effects of winds and tides. Remember to walk slowly and be patient. Some beaches are better than others for beach combing, you can find out about the best ones on the Internet.

## WARNING!

Take care! Don't ever turn your back on the tide or you may be caught out by an unexpectedly large and powerful wave that could sweep you out to sea. Be

careful about what you handle. Some objects are sharp or dangerous. Watch out for the tar and oil that coats others – it's a nightmare to get off your hands and clothes. And if you find a jellyfish, just look at it. It might still be alive and sting you!

GRRR!

# G'DAY MITE! BE AUSTRALIAN FOR A DAY

**HOW TO DO IT**

Familiarize yourself with Australian words and phrases and slip them into your conversation as much as possible. This quick quiz should help you to wrap your brain around a few...

## I DUNNY

a) a task you've just completed b) a dozy person c) an outdoor toilet

## II BERKO

a) a dozy person b) angry c) a male Koala bear

## III ARVO
a) afternoon b) half c) the Australian Royal Air Force

## IV STORM STICK
a) a lightning conductor b) an umbrella c) a Tazer

## V DUNNY BUDGIE
a) a fly b) a small brown bird c) a small brown bird which is dead

## VI GRUNDIES
a) a bad mood b) people who live underground c) underwear

## VII LIKE A RAT UP A DRAINPIPE
a) stuck b) quick c) dangerous

## VIII RATTLE YOUR DAGS
a) Hurry up b) Take your pets for walk c) Sort out your cutlery drawer

Answers 1 c) 2 b) as in 'throw a berko!' 3 a) 4 b) 5 a) because they hang around dunnies 6 c) after Reg Grundy, a well known Australian TV star 7 c) 8 a).

Become addicted to these delicious Aussie food favourites...

## PIE FLOATERS: Meat pies floating upside down in bowls of mushy peas covered with tomato sauce, or 'dead horse' as Aussies call it.

## TIM TAM SLAMS: Bite off opposite corners of a chocolate-covered Tim Tam biscuit, or similar British choccy bikky, such as a Penguin bar, put one end in a cup of tea or coffee, then suck the drink through the middle until the biscuit collapses, at which point you stuff the whole messy lot in your mouth.

## VEGEMITE (AUSTRALIAN MARMITE): Squeeze it through the holes in Vita-Weat crackers to make brown 'worms'.

# BUILD A WILDERNESS SURVIVAL SHELTER FROM NATURAL MATERIALS

**Important note:** This sort of shelter won't work in wild places like the Sahara desert or the North Pole, as you will have a very long walk before finding any suitable natural building materials (and by the time you do find them you'll have forgotten what you wanted them for in the first place).

WHAT YOU NEED: ↓

• string, a sharp knife, an axe, plus tenacity, ingenuity and unlimited reserves of 'raw pluck' (available from all good DIY stores).

ALL OTHER ITEMS ARE IN HERE

## Choose your shelter site. Places to avoid include...

a) Marshy areas or river banks where swarms of insects will eat your face off.

b) Narrow valleys or ravines where damp, misty air will chill you to the bone and flash floods will wash you away.

c) Mountain tops where storm-force winds will blow your face off.

d) Places where dead tree branches or loose rocks will fall on you and squash you flatter than a light-crust pizza.

e) Busy shopping malls, airport terminals and major motorways.

An ideal site would be one with plenty of spruce trees around as they are perfect shelter building material. These trees are the 'evergreen' sort that are used for Grand National jumps, Christmas trees and making the paper on which these words are printed. Their leafy branches make excellent waterproof roofing material and, if you do happen to forget your string, you can also use their roots for tying things.

**FASCINATING FACT:** There are some spruce trees in Sweden that are a stonking 9,500 years old! So please, don't use them for your shelter (they don't grow on trees, you know).

There are lots of ways to build shelters. One of easiest is to erect is a 'lean-to'. What to do: First clear away anything which may cause you discomfort during your stay in the shelter e.g. sharp stones, spiky twigs, dead porcupines, unexploded Second World War bombs etc.

If there's a large boulder handy, lean a long strong branch against it with one end resting on the ground. This is your 'ridge pole'.

DAD, I'VE GOT A LITTLE BOULDER

WELL DONE, SON. IT'S TIME YOU TOUGHENED UP!

Lean small branches against each side of the long branch at 45-degree angles. Tie them to the long branch and push their opposite ends into the earth. If there isn't a boulder handy cut a couple of strong branches with forked endings and push them into the ground about two metres apart. For your ridge pole, lay a horizontal branch across the top of these uprights and tie it to the forked ends. Next, lean smaller branches against the horizontal branch and tie them to. Now push more branches into the earth to make the side walls. If possible, make sure the back of your lean-to is facing the prevailing wind. Alternatively, you may like to build a couple of shelters that face each other with a fire in between them. Of course, if there are a couple of trees handy you can always wedge your 'ridge pole' between them.

Now 'thatch' your skeleton. Collect lots of leafy branches, ferns, twigs, moss, and clumps of grass. Lay them on the branches to make a thick covering that will keep out wind, rain (and the horrid forest demons which will suck out your eyeballs given half a chance). And don't forget that spruce-tree branches make excellent waterproof 'thatching' material.

If you do use leaves and grass, don't forget to place plenty of sticks on top to stop it being blown away. Finally, slap great handfuls of mud all over your 'thatch' (or, if you're feeling playful, all over your dad).

**SAFETY TIP:** Chopping branches and sticks is a dangerous business so get your dad to carry out this hazardous work. If he complains, just tell him you're promoting him to 'branch manager' and the power-crazy twit will be chuffed to bits.

Finally, carpet the floor of your shelter with leaves.

**Important**! Whilst preparing to build your shelter don't get too fussed over things like colour schemes, scenic views or where you're going to put the settee, or you may end up freezing to death before you've laid the first twig.

# EAT A ZOMBIE'S FACE: IT'S A PIECE OF CAKE!

This terribly gruesome, but completely scrumptious, severed zombie head is tons of fun to make ... and tons of fun to eat, too.

ANOTHER EYEBALL, VICAR?

The instructions below are for a basic zombie head but, as you're baking and making, you'll soon realize how hideously creative you can get with this ghoulish project, letting your imagination out of its dingy, cobweb-filled dungeon and sending it scampering round in search of horrendously yucky, but totally yummy, finishing touches for your masterpiece.

The basic ingredients for the head come in three parts: a sturdy cake mixture to bake and carve the head from, buttercream icing to cover it with and soft fondant icing to sculpt the details from. You'll be making the cake and the buttercream icing yourself but you can buy the soft fondant icing at your local supermarket.

# HOW TO MAKE THE CAKES FOR THE HEAD

**WHAT YOU NEED**

**KITCHEN KIT:**

• Four round cake tins: two 20 cm and two 15 cm ones
• A whisk
• A mixing bowl
• An electric food mixer
• A cake leveller*

*A sharp knife will do instead.

**INGREDIENTS**

- 2 boxes of cake mix
- 1 cup of flour
- 1 cup of granulated sugar
- A dash of salt
- 1 cup of sour cream
- 1 cup of water
- 3 whole eggs
- 1 tablespoon of flavouring*

* Of course, you can choose what flavour the cake will be: scrumptious chocolate, repulsive raspberry, lurid lemon, (gruesome garlic, horrendous horse meat) ... it's up to you!

**WHAT TO DO**

**1** Blend your cake mix, flour, sugar and salt together in a bowl using your whisk.

**2** Put your sour cream, water, eggs* and flavouring in an electric food mixer bowl then add half of the cake mix, flour, sugar and salt mix.

77

\* It's probably a good idea to remove the shells from the eggs before you add them to the mix as you don't want your cake to be too crunchy.

**3** Blend them together using your whisk then add the rest of the ingredients and blend them again.

**4** Mix the whole lot together for 2 minutes using the electric mixer.

**5** Pour your zombie mixture into your cake tins.

**6** Put them in an oven heated to 300 degrees and bake them for 30 minutes.

**7** Let them cool completely after baking then thinly slice off the cake tops so they're nice and level.

**8** When they're cool, put them in the freezer.

# HOW TO MAKE THE BUTTERCREAM ICING

**WHAT YOU NEED** ↘
Kitchen kit: a mixing bowl and wooden spoon
Ingredients:

- 140 g/5 oz of butter
- 280 g/10 oz of icing sugar
- 1-2 tablespoons of milk
- A few drops of food colouring

## WHAT TO DO ↘

**1** Use your wooden spoon to beat the butter in a large bowl until it's nice and soft. Do this in a warm room.

**2** Add half of your icing sugar to the butter and beat it until it's got a really smooth texture.

**3** Add the rest of the icing sugar and one tablespoon of the milk and beat the mixture until it's even smoother and creamier.

**4** You're going to be smearing this mixture all over your zombie head so, if it seems a bit stiff for this, add a little more milk to make it more spreadable.

**5** Stir in the food colouring until you've got a nice even shade.

## NOW IT'S TIME TO MAKE THE ZOMBIE HEAD!

**WHAT YOU NEED** ↘
**KITCHEN KIT:**

- Spatulas
- Fondant tools
- A board to roll your fondant on
- A fondant rolling pin
- Food-safe paintbrushes
- Small containers to mix your food colour "paints" in

**INGREDIENTS**

- Your four 'head cakes'
- Buttercream icing
- Fondant
- Gel food colouring

- Clear vanilla extract to mix your colours with
- Gummy eyeball sweets
- Anything else you can think of

## WHAT TO DO

**1** Put on your mad scientist wig and glasses and laugh insanely (optional).

**2** Take your four cakes out of the freezer. Put the two 15-cm ones on top of the two 20-cm ones with a layer of buttercream between each of them.

**3** Now for the carving! Using a really sharp knife carve out the shape of your zombie's head. Start with basic head shape then sculpt out hollows for the eyeballs to rest in. Next carve the nose and mouth shapes.

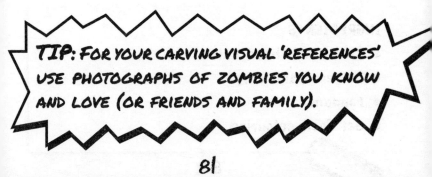

TIP: FOR YOUR CARVING VISUAL 'REFERENCES' USE PHOTOGRAPHS OF ZOMBIES YOU KNOW AND LOVE (OR FRIENDS AND FAMILY).

**4** Using your cake spatula, give your zombie's head an all-over coat of buttercream.

**5** Use your rolling pin and board to roll out a sheet of soft white fondant icing.

**6** Carefully cover the whole head with it.

**7** Use your fingers to smooth out the fondant on the head.

**8** Now use your sculpting tools to shape out your zombie's facial features in detail.

**9** Now make your zombie some fondant ears and attach with buttercream, carving in their fine detail after you've stuck them on.

**10** Stick the zombie's gummy eyeball sweets in the hollows you carved out for them.

Run out of the room, never wanting to see your creation again, just as Dr Frankenstein did when he first looked his 'creature' in the eye (optional).

**11** Now you can get really creative as you start to use your cake-decorating kit, accessories and paint to render your severed zombie head as loathsome as you like.

Here are a few things you might like to enhance your zombie head with but you can probably think of tons more: sugar-lump teeth (brown and white), fresh strawberry buboes with marzipan pus oozing from them, chocolate sauce scars...

And finally a ... serving suggestion! How about presenting your severed head in pool of blood made from gelatin, icing sugar and red food-colouring in which chocolate spiders scurry, sugar mice nibble and jelly worms wriggle!

# MAKE AN INDIAN TEEPEE YOU CAN CAMP OUT IN

In the days when nomadic Native American Indian tribes such as the Comanche, Dakota and Sioux followed gigantic herds of bison across the American Great Plains they had to have a house that could quickly and easily be taken down and put up again. So they came up with the idea of the teepee. A teepee is a simple, cone-shaped frame made from wooden poles covered with animal skins, birch bark or, more recently, canvas. Teepees kept the Native American Indians warm in cold, snowy winters, dry in torrential rain and cool in the summer. Nor did they get blown away by the ferocious winds that blasted the Great Plains. And of course, with teepees, the Native Americans were always able to move house at the drop of a bison-fur rug, quite literally! Just as you will when you've made yours! And don't forget that as well as something you can go camping in or just play in, your teepee can also be a brilliant prop if you decide to do get involved in the exciting living-history described on page 203.

84

However, whatever you do, don't call your teepee a 'wigwam', as that's the Native American Indian name for a dome-shaped dwelling.

NON-SMOKING OR SMOKING? It's your decision. The other great thing about Native American teepees was that it was possible to have a fire inside them. Their shape, combined with the draught that came in from the bottom and went out through the hole at the top, created a 'chimney effect' which meant that smoke from the fire in the middle of the circular living space disappeared through the hole rather than choking everyone to death. But if you do decide to build your teepee with 'smoke flaps' as they're known it will make the job a bit more complicated. It's up to you.

And finally a quick word about 'BIGGING UP' V. 'DOWNSIZING'. The measurements are for a big, 3-metre-high teepee which will be large enough for you, your dad and the dog to hunker down in for the rest of your lives when you've been banished from the house for being too noisy, untidy, rough, or

85

constantly sniffing your own bottom (that'll be the dog, not you and your dad). However, feel free to adapt the measurements, instructions and materials to make a smaller or even simpler teepee that suits your requirements, time and budget perfectly. In fact, if you wish you can make a really small teepee for your Lego Comanche Indians (or extremely tiny granny) to live in.

## WHAT YOU NEED ↘

### TOOLS:
- Big stonky fabric-cutting scissors
- A tape measure
- A saw
- A size 16 or 18 sewing needle
- Heavy-duty thread
- Paintbrushes
- A pencil
- String
- A sharpened stick

## MATERIALS

• A sheet of canvas twice as long as it's wide. The best sort to use is 8 oz or 12 oz white cotton canvas. However, if you've decided to make a small, simple 'summer' teepee, which isn't meant to last for ever, you can use a blanket or sheeting material. Alternatively you may wish to make your teepee from bison skin (available at all good safari parks).

- 14 poles which are at least a metre longer than your canvas is wide — but again, you don't need poles which are that long or quite as many if you're going for the 'teepee-lite' option.
- Strong rope, cord or washing line
- Paints to decorate your teepee with

## WHAT TO DO

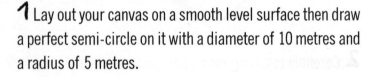

1 Lay out your canvas on a smooth level surface then draw a perfect semi-circle on it with a diameter of 10 metres and a radius of 5 metres.

"What!" you say, "I'm not Leonardo da blinking Vinci, you know! How do you expect me to do that?" Well it's simple. All you have to do to draw your perfect semi-circle is to make a mega-compass. Which is easy! All you need is your sharpened stick, a piece of string and a pencil. Tie the pencil to one end of the string and the stick to the other. Push the stick into the ground exactly halfway along the canvas's long edge. Now stretch out the string and mark out a semi-circle as large as you possibly can so that you don't waste canvas.

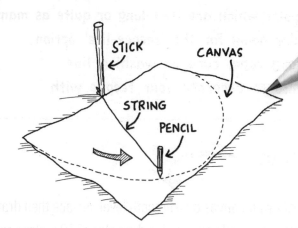

**2** Carefully cut along the pencil line until you end up with a semi-circle of canvas.

**3** Now, following the diagram on the next page, cut out:

a) Your 2 smoke flaps – these are optional, as mentioned before you'll only need them if you're planning on having a fire in your teepee.

b) Your semi-circular door openings which will form a complete circle when they're joined – these are also optional, but only if you're planning on not actually going inside your teepee!

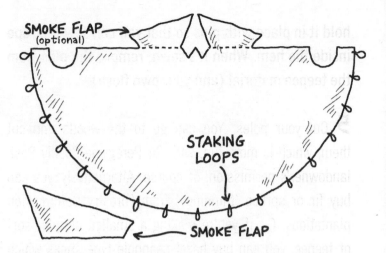

SMOKE FLAP→
(optional)

STAKING
LOOPS

← SMOKE FLAP

**4** Ahem! Now it's time for some sewing, unless you're making a really simple teepee, in which case ignore this bit. Using your needle and thread, sew a strong hem into the circular side of your canvas, incorporating a rope or washing line. Your hem is there to:

a) Prevent your teepee edges from fraying. (Just like your lips are there to stop the edges of your mouth from fraying.)

b) To give you something to attach ropes loops to so that your teepee can be pegged down to stop it being blown away on windy days.

✳ **A note about hemming**
Fold the teepee edge over the rope or washing line then

90

hold it in place with pins so that you can sew the rope inside the hem. When it's sewn, remove the pins from the teepee material (and your own flesh).

**5** Cut your poles. You can go to the woods and cut them, which is more fun, with Sir Peregrine Poshly-Posh landowner's permission, of course. Alternatively, you can buy fir or spruce 'thinnings' from Forestry Commission plantations. Or, if you're making a smaller, simpler sort of teepee, you can buy hazel beanpole-type sticks which have been coppiced i.e. they've been harvested from living trees as part of a woodland management scheme. You could also buy thick bamboo poles but some think this is an environmentally unfriendly thing to do (especially pandas). The main thing about your poles is that they should be as straight as you can possibly get them and nice and smooth so they don't rub against the fabric and make holes in it.

**6** Now it's time for the exciting part: putting up your teepee frame! First place three poles on the cover laid flat on the ground as shown in this diagram. This will be your 'lifting tripod'. Tie the poles where they cross with 10 cm of rope. Use a clove hitch followed by a reef knot for this.

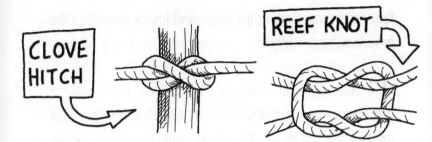

**CLOVE HITCH**

**REEF KNOT**

**7** Lift your poles so they splay into a tripod shape then push them into the ground so that they're stable. Once the tripod is up, add all but one of the other the poles into the circle, pushing them into the earth as you do so.

**8** Now get your canvas onto your teepee frame. To do this use the last pole, which is known as a lifting pole. Tie the lifting pole to the canavas at the little flap marked on the top middle of the diagram. Then lift your canvas into place, positioning your lifting pole opposite where your door's going to be.

**9** Now wrap the canvas around the teepee and fasten it with the pegs/clips.

**10** Splay out the teepee poles a bit more to make sure the canvas is stretched nice and tight on them then push your tent pegs through the rope loops and knock them into the ground with your mallet.

**11** Now you can decorate your teepee. First wet the canvas so that it's stretched really tight then choose your images and patterns. You could copy traditional Indian teepee decorations from pictures in books or the Internet or you might like to make up your own designs including things like handprints.

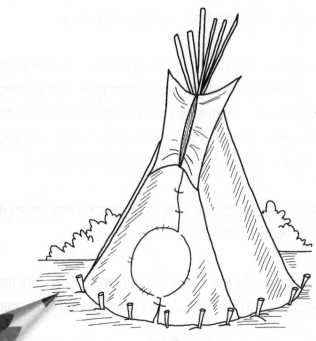

# TOO DAFT FOR WORDS! (WELL, ALMOST!) DRAW A STRIP CARTOON

TELL A STORY USING WORDS AND PICTURES BY DRAWING A STRIP CARTOON. IT'S HARD WORK. BUT IT'S TONS OF FUN!

## WHAT YOU NEED ↓

- Lots of patience, determination and imagination
- Cheap white sketching paper for practising
- Good quality white cartridge paper for your finished cartoon
- A variety of pencil grades such as HB, B and 2B. These letters and numbers indicate the hardness/softness and blackness of the graphite and clay mix which makes the marks on the paper. H stands for Hardness and B stands for Blackness.
- Good quality coloured pencils or felt tips
- A pencil sharpener
- An eraser – the 'putty' sort are good
- Black ink felt-tip pens with points of varying thickness

• A matte: this is a frame cut from a piece of card which enables you to draw the rectangular borders for each frame of your strip cartoon quite easily. It can be made using a small surgeon's knife known as a scalpel (the surgeon isn't small, the knife is), a metal straight-edge ruler and a set square.

**Really important safety note:** Get your dad to make the matte as it's a dangerous thing to. He might like to make several mattes of differing sizes to vary the appearance of your cartoon strip.

WHAT TO DO

A: DEVELOP YOUR CARTOONING STYLE

**1** Wash your hands before you start drawing. You don't want grubby fingerprints all over your work!

95

**2** Study your favourite strip cartoons. But don't copy them! It's fine to be inspired by professional cartoon strips, but copying them will only limit your own potential cartooning style.

**3** As you draw, try not to support your hand on your wrist like you do when you're writing. This will give your hand the freedom to make interesting shapes with lines that 'flow'.

**4** Practice some doodles to build up your confidence. Also draw some circles, oblongs, rectangles and wavy lines.

**5** Make your first drawings with pale lines. In other words. don't press too hard with your pencil.

**6** You're recreating a 3D world in a 2D form so teach yourself to draw three-dimensional shapes using shadows and perspective. Now try stretching or squashing the 3D shapes.

## B: CREATE SOME CHARACTERS

Use an artists mannequin i.e. a wooden figure with moveable

96

limbs. This will help you to create 'active' characters in various positions such as running, walking, sitting down, crawling etc. Practice drawing faces and hands.

TIP: DRAWING 'CARTOON' HANDS WITH THREE FINGERS AND A THUMB IS EASIER THAN DOING THE NORMAL SORT.

Think about the clothes your characters are wearing. Are they smart, weird, scruffy...? Think about their hair. Is it tidy, slick, ruffled, partly hidden by a hat...? Your characters will need to have expressions: happy, angry, surprised, sad, dim ... that sort of thing. Exaggerate your characters' features to make them more cartoon-like.

TIP: USE A MIRROR AND PULL FACES IN IT TO GET AN IDEA OF HOW THESE EXPRESSIONS SHOULD LOOK (BUT AVOID FRIGHTENING YOURSELF TO DEATH).
OR, EVEN BETTER, GET YOUR DAD TO ACT AS YOUR MODEL, ADAPTING ALL SORTS OF POSES AND FACIAL EXPRESSION. (WHAT DO YOU MEAN HE'S ONLY GOT ONE EXPRESSION?)

## C: CREATE A LITTLE 'ADVENTURE' FOR YOUR CHARACTERS

THE ADVENTURES OF JIM THE BADGER

**1** Let your imagination off its lead and take it for a scamper around a fantasy world.

**2** Keep your story simple. And don't try to put too much detail in your first drawings.

**3** When you've roughly sketched out your story in pencil, add speech bubbles and thought bubbles.

*TIP: SLOPPY LETTERING CAN RUIN A GOOD CARTOON. DRAW FAINT PENCIL LINES INSIDE THE BUBBLES TO KEEP YOUR LETTERING TIDY. YOU CAN RUB THESE OUT LATER. REMEMBER TO SPACE THE WORDS EQUALLY.*

**4** Once you're happy with what you've drawn and written, go over the pencil lines with an ink pen. Carefully rub out any traces of the pencil line.

**5** Colour in your characters and the backgrounds if you want to.

**6** Show your cartoons to friends and family. Accept their 'constructive' comments and think about them when you create your next strip.

**7** Be observant as you go about your daily life and look for things that'll give you ideas for your next cartoon strips.

**8** Never stop learning and developing your style.

And finally ... make sure you're enjoying yourself. If you are it will show in your work.

# LEARN TO YODEL LIKE A LONELY COWBOY (OR A LONELY COW)

Yodelling began when neighbours and friends in mountainous places such as the Swiss Alps, Bavaria (and Norfolk) had trouble communicating with each other because their houses were separated by deep valleys or gigantic glaciers. This, of course, made chatting over the garden fence or asking to borrow a cup of ewe's milk really difficult, especially as telephones hadn't been invented. The mountain dwellers overcame this problem by developing an unusual shouting style, which sounds rather like a pig gargling with jelly, in which they yelled things like, 'Your St Bernard has just eaten my edelweiss!' or 'Could you help me extricate this cuckoo from my clock', in wobbly 'up-and-down' voices which could quite clearly be heard in neighbouring valleys. And of course, the sound of this jelly-gargling technique was even more enhanced by the fact that the sounds would echo around the mountains and valleys (and the yodellers wouldn't know if they were listening to their own echo or the reply from their neighbour).

100

In the 1800s, the yodellers began doing a musical version of the jelly gargling while leaping around slapping their own bottoms, playing accordions and wearing ridiculous leather shorts. When European mountain folk emigrated to America along with their yodels, it was soon taken up by cowboys as entertainment (or self-torture) while they drove humongous herds of cattle across (extremely flat) American plains to the stockyards where they would then be slaughtered and turned into burgers and dog meat (the cows, not the cowboys).

## WHAT TO DO

**1** Get inspired: There are loads of videos on the Internet you could look up.

**2** Get to understand 'pitch'. High-pitched sounds are ones such as might be made by a squirrel which has just impaled itself on a blackberry briar, and low-pitched notes are ones like those made by hippopotamuses grumbling about the cost of mud.

**3** Discover your two voices. One, which is known as your 'head voice', is that with which you sing high-pitched, 'falsetto' notes and the other, your 'chest voice' is the one you use for low-pitched notes.

**4** Now sing a long, held-out, 'extended' note during which you rapidly and repeatedly change the pitch from your 'head voice' to your 'chest voice'. What you're doing is exaggerating the 'catch' or 'break'* in your voice where the difference between high and low notes is deliberately emphasized.

**NB: If you're a 12- or 13-year-old boy you won't even have to try to do this as it will happen naturally because you're undergoing the growing-up voice-breaking process known as puberty (or you might be turning into a werewolf).**

*Professional non-yodelling singers do their best to eliminate this 'catch' by constantly making smooth transitions from low to high notes and vice-versa.

**5** Now yodel, 'Yodel – Ay – EEE – Oooo', singing the EEE bit in your 'head voice' and other bits in your 'chest voice'.

**6** Go somewhere really echoey such as a railway tunnel (preferably disused), mountain top, or your bathroom and listen your yodel bouncing around.

**7** Sing along with all those yodel recordings you found in step 1.

**8** And finally, now that you and your dad have learned to yodel, it's time to get the whole family involved. Then, once you've become a team of crack yodellers why not try out your new-found skills in public places such train carriages where your yodels will drown out the sound of noisy twits on their mobile phones or in the aisles of your local supermarket where you can yodel back and forth suggestions for that night's dinner.

HAPPY YODELLING!

# GROW A LITTLE GARDEN OF HORRORS A CARNIVOROUS PLANT TERRARIUM (OR, IF YOU HAPPEN TO BE A FLY ... 'TERROR'ARIUM!)

Carnivorous plants are totally awesome and weird! If you want to witness scenes of scintillating savagery where Venus's-flytraps clamp their evil spiky jaws on careless crickets, pitcher plants lure unwary ants onto slippery slopes of death, and sundew plants snare hapless aphids with their sticky leaves, then this is definitely for you!

Carnivorous plants normally grow in places where the soil contains very few nutrients so, over thousands of years, the wicked little midge-munchers have learned to supplement their diets with 'takeaways', snacking on passing bugs, butterflies, spiders, wasps, midges, moths, gnats and crickets and, very occasionally, even on small lizards, rodents, birds (cows and lost children). Actually, despite what horror movies (and children's authors), would have you believe, carnivorous plants don't actually attack people or large animals ... thank goodness!

So, what are you waiting for? Forget that nasty, environmentally unfriendly fly spray. Get rid of your bluebottles and greenfly the natural way, make a little garden of horrors!

DO YOU EVER WISH YOU'D LEARNED HOW TO READ?

VENUS'S FLY TRAP

▷ **Fascinating fact:** The Nepethene pitcher plant traps and 'eats' frogs but its digestive juices can't handle the skin on the frogs' feet. So when it's finished dinner, it leaves behind a little pair of frog 'slippers'!

## WHAT YOU NEED ↘

● Activated charcoal: this is charcoal that's been processed to make it very porous and absorbent. It will not only eliminate any toxic chemicals which might harm your gruesome green gobblers, but will also remove the bad pongs from your little garden of horrors e.g. stinky spider, manky midge.

● Some distilled water: this is water which has been boiled then condensed to remove the impurities from it — carnivorous plants are very fussy about what they slurp and don't like to drink tap water (or, quite sensibly, cola).

● A glass or see-through container: the safest thing to use is one of the plastic all-purpose ones which are sold at pet shops as homes for fish, hamsters, tarantulas, carnivorous plants (and homeless woodlice). They usually come with a lid (which comes in very useful if your carnivores ever try to make a break for freedom). The lid has a sliding or hinged top opening for ventilation, feeding etc.

- Sphagnum peat moss: this moss comes from the sort of swamps and bogs where carnivorous plants grow in the wild.
- Gravel, little pebbles or even crushed plant pots to provide drainage.
- A bog-type soil mixture. Your 'monstrous-munchers' like soil that is low in nutrients and high in acids – in other words, something that makes them feel at home. Mix equal amounts of sterilized soil, peat moss and vermiculite together to create a soil to suit them. Peat moss is dried, decayed vegetation matter and vermiculite is a natural mineral which expands when it gets hot. You can also add in perlite, silica sand, pine needles and bark (but only if you feel like imitating a dog).
- Some carnivorous plants, of course, but we'll come to them in a tick.
- Some victims, such as crickets, flies, ants, greenfly, midges (or Shetland ponies).

**WHAT TO DO**

Before you begin this bit remind yourself that you're attempting to create a miniature ecosystem that perfectly mimics the environment where your ferocious little fronds grow in the wild.

**1** Spread a 2.5-cm layer of gravel or small pebbles across the bottom of your terrarium.

**2** Cover the gravel with about a centimetre of the activated charcoal.

**3** Cover the gravel and charcoal with the sphagnum peat moss. This will prevent your next layer, the soil, from dropping into the gravel and making muddy gloop. Add distilled water to the peat moss until it turns black.

**4** Cover the peat moss with a 3.5-cm layer of your soil mixture bark, stones and pine needles.

**5** Now place your terrarium in dappled light where the temperature averages 65 to 75 degrees during the day and

55 to 65 degrees at night. Carnivorous plants don't like dim light, very low, or very high temperatures or draughts (but they do enjoy the occasional game of table tennis). You could set up a fluorescent light strip over the terrarium to make sure they get sufficient light and heat.

## NOW FOR THE GRUESOME-GREEN-GOBBLERS: VENUS'S-FLYTRAP

The best way to start off your terrarium is with just one sort of carnivorous plant then add others as you become more experienced and knowledgeable about caring for them. And the best beginner's midge-muncher is the Venus's-flytrap (or 'Jaws' as it's known to its friends).

Venus's-flytraps grow naturally in the Carolina swamps of North America and they really are the great white sharks of the carnivorous-plant world with their fearsome spiky fangs that dramatically clamp their prey, making escape impossible. They're also quite tough and relatively easy to look after (and don't need to be house trained or taken for walks in the park).

# PLANTING AND CARING FOR YOUR VENUS'S-FLYTRAPS

**WHAT TO DO**

**1** Make a little space in the 'soil' and put your Venus's-flytrap in it, making sure the roots are well bedded in.

**2** You must now wet the bed. No, not like that! Like this. Water in your plants with distilled water. Try not to splash water on your flytrap's leaves as it may cause disease. Keep the soil in your terrarium fairly moist but definitely not soggy.

**3** Cover the terrarium with a see-through Perspex lid leaving about 10 percent open as a ventilation gap.

**Important:** If all sides of your terrarium become covered with condensation, open the ventilation gap some more. Water around the plants and try not to wet the leaves excessively.

**4** Pruning, cleaning and tidying: Remove dead leaves from your meat-eaters and pull moss away from their stems.

Clean the inner windows of your terrarium using damp kitchen roll but never use window cleaner!
And now, it's ... **FEEDING TIME!**

Amazingly, you only need to feed your Venus's-flytraps once a month. But the dramatic spectacle of them munching an insect is certainly worth waiting for! Feed them living or dead insects such baby crickets, flies and ants but whatever you do, don't give them live caterpillars or the little wrigglers will simply chew their way to freedom! Small dead caterpillars are fine (and so is the occasional leg of roast lamb). If you feed your Venus's-flytrap a dead insect it won't close tightly over it, so you will need to squeeze the trap generally and move the food around so the poor carnivorous dimwit 'thinks' the insect is alive. But take lots of care when doing this (or it will have your hand off in a flash).

➤ **Important:** Don't deliberately tease your flytrap, getting it snapping away like a rabid bull terrier. Even five or six openings and closings will exhaust the poor little monster and kill it.

THIS IS YOUR ANTIPASTA!

I'M FULL OF ANT'ICIPATION!

WELL I THINK IT'S ALL VERY ANTI-ANT!

## THE REALLY GRUESOME BIT

Of course, to successfully feed your Venus's-flytraps and thoroughly enjoy witnessing their macabre munching, it's really important that you understand how the gruesome thing works. So prepare yourself – it's very horrible!

On the inner surface of the Venus's-flytrap's leaves are tiny hairs that act as a trigger to snap its jaws shut. So, when an insect or spider crawls along the flytrap's leaf and touches one of these hairs ... nothing happens! However, if that spider or insect touches another hair within the next 20 seconds, the trap snaps SHUT! This brilliant system means that the flytrap isn't forever closing when just any old thing touches it, and therefore it doesn't waste its valuable energy chomping stuff like leaves, twigs, seeds (bus tickets and old shirt buttons) which have no nutritional value. Now, who on earth though that up?

When the hairs are triggered by something genuinely noshable, the two 'lobes' of the leaves snap shut in less than a second. The trap doesn't close all the way at first – it stays open for a few seconds. It's thought that this is to allow really small insects to escape because they don't provide enough food (or because the Venus's-flytrap feels sorry for them). And if the flytrap does happen to accidentally catch a stone, or a nut, it will reopen about twelve hours later and 'spit' it out.

PHTTT!

Once the flytrap has closed tightly over the victim, it makes an air-tight seal which keeps digestive fluids in and bacteria out. The digestive juices, just like the ones in a human stomach, then get to work on little Jiminy Cricket, dissolving all his insides, but not his tough outer skeleton. This whole process takes between five and twelve days then the trap reopens and the leftovers are washed out by rain or blown away. Amazing!

# HERE ARE SOME OTHER BUG-BITERS YOU CAN GROW

The sundew, scientific name drosera, looks like a beautiful flower or a very cool-looking stem with dewdrops all over it, but the dewdrops are actually mucilage (like mucous) at the ends of the tentacles that it uses to trap its prey. (Sneaky or what!) The sundew primarily preys on insects and waits for the insects to land on the inviting flowers. The insect gets stuck in the mucilage and then gets digested. There are about 170 different sorts of sundew plants and they grow naturally in Africa, Venezuela and Australia.

The pitcher plant comes in all shapes and sizes, and grows around the world in different variations and species. The North American pitcher plant looks like a rolled-up leaf forming a tube. Inside the tube a gel substance traps insects that make their way into the tube. Some species of pitcher plants have a fly-paper type of trap rather than a tube trap, which is known as a pitfall trap. Some pitcher plants look like flowers, some like stems, and some look like leaves.

# BUILD YOUR VERY OWN WEAPON OF MASS DESTRUCTION. A WORKING MEDIEVAL SIEGE ENGINE OR TREBUCHET

There's history, physics, engineering (and a fair bit of gratuitous violence) in this exciting project (so it's especially suitable for girls). In medieval times, before the invention of gunpowder, in an age when life was said to be nasty, brutish and short (what do you mean, 'Just like my Dad!'?), warring armies used trebuchets. These stonking great siege machines hurled rocks, flaming tar-covered boulders, diseased bodies and all sorts of other 'interesting' stuff into enemy cities with the ease of a giant lobbing a radish over a garden wall. This project tells you how to build one of these stupendous siege machines – possibly not quite big enough to hurl a putrid cow into your next-door-neighbour's fishpond, but certainly with enough whumph to clobber their back door with a rubber chicken.

It should take you about two hours to make (or two years, if you're all fingers and thumbs).

## WHAT YOU NEED ↘

TOOLS:

- A hammer
- A saw
- A screwdriver
- Some needle-nose pliers for handling small objects (and needle noses)
- Some wood glue
- A file
- Scissors
- A drill and drill bits
- Sandpaper
- Metal cutters

BITS AND BOBS ↘

- A heavy lump of clay, a rock or a piece of metal for your counter weight – or you could use a couple of batteries taped together or some coins tightly tied inside a plastic bag. Use your ingenuity and improvisational skills to come up with something original.
- A metal bar at least 130 mm long: this will support the trebuchet's counterweight so it must be quite strong, something like a toy car axle, coat hanger metal or screwdriver blade would do.
- Small screws
- Small nails
- 2 screw eyes
- Some wire or freezer-bag ties
- Gaffa tape
- 1 metre of string
- A small piece of cloth, about 150 mm square
- A small plastic bag
- 1 strip of thin cardboard 300 mm x 180 mm

• **Wood:** The best size wood to use is about 25 x 13 mm. You'll need about 2 metres of it. You'll also need a square piece of flat wood about 130 x 160 mm and 6 mm thick.

## WHAT TO DO

**1** Cut your 25 x 13 mm wood to the following lengths:
One 400-mm piece for the swing arm
Two 300-mm pieces for the long base pieces
Two 250-mm pieces for the uprights
Three 125-mm pieces for the cross-pieces on the base

**2** Draw a diagonal line across the flat piece of wood from one corner to the other then cut along this line to make the two triangular pieces that'll support and strengthen your uprights.

**3** Mark a line 75 mm along on the 300-mm pieces of wood then place a 250-mm piece of wood at this mark so the two pieces create a right angle (or a right mess, if you're useless at woodwork).

75mm

**4** Put one of your triangles onto these two pieces so that its right angle lies exactly on top of their right angle then glue it in place, strengthening the join with a few screws or nails.

**5** Repeat the process with the other 250-mm and 300-mm pieces and the remaining triangle so that you create a mirror image of the arrangement you created in step 4. You have now made the uprights of your trebuchet.

**6** Stand your uprights with the triangle on the outside then glue the 125-mm cross-pieces onto the base, one at each end and the remaining one butting up to verticals on the longer side of the horizontals. You've now made the trebuchet's main frame.

**7** Mark a spot 25 mm below the top of each upright on its outside face. Drill a hole big enough to push your metal bar through at each spot. But don't push the bar through yet.

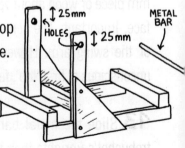

25mm

HOLES

25mm

METAL BAR

**8** Screw one of your screw eyes into one end of your 400-mm piece of wood.

**9** Make three marks on this wood, each 25-mm apart, starting with one 75-mm from the screw eye end. Drill them so that your metal bar slides through them easily, but is not too loose. If the wood swings round the bar smoothly, you've got it just right.

**10** Hammer a nail into the opposite end of the 400-mm piece of wood at a slight angle.

**11** Snip or file off the nail's head to allow the string to slip off it easily when your trebuchet lobs its missile.

**12** Screw in another screw eye into the same end of the 400-mm piece of wood about 12 mm from the end on its narrowest face. Important: The screw eye should be on the lower face of the swing arm. However, if you wish to knock yourself unconscious at first 'lob', feel free to screw it onto the top face.

**13** Slide the metal bar through the hole in one of the trebuchet's uprights then through the first hole in the swing arm and finally through the hole in the other upright. Make sure your arm swings nice and smoothly and doesn't wobble. BTW: The same applies to the trebuchet's arm!

**14** Put your counterweight in a small plastic bag. Use plenty of gaffa tape to securely attach the wire or freezer-bag tie to the weight.

**15** Attach your counterweight to the screw eye in the opposite end of the swing arm to the angled nail by threading the wire or freezer-bag tie through it then twisting it really tightly. The last thing you want is your counterweight dropping off and squashing a dozen of your soldiers flat just when you're in the middle of besieging.

SWINGING ARM

HOLES

NA

HOOK

HOOK

COUNTERWEIGHT

**16** Now for the ammo pouch. Cut two pieces of string at least 45 cm long. Fold your cloth in half and tie each end with a string so it looks like a hammock for a hibernating hamster.

**17** Fix a wire loop to the end of one of your lengths of string.

**18** Attach your pouch to the trebuchet arm by hooking the wire loop over the bent nail and tying the end of the other length of string to the screw eye beneath it. The wire loop is meant to slide off the nail when you fire your evil weapon of mass destruction. Trim the strings so that the pouch is about 30 cm from the angled nail.

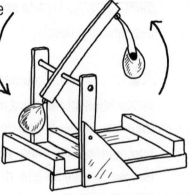

**19** You must now make something for your pouch and ammo to slide along when your trebuchet fires. Do this by folding up 25 mm of the edges of your thin cardboard to make a chute the same length as your trebuchet. Glue it onto the trebuchet's three 125-mm crossbars.

**20** Ooh, ooh! It's lift-off time! First you must choose your ammo, or projectile as it's known technically. This could be a lump of clay, a malteser (or even the rotting corpse of a tadpole).

**21** Place your ammo in the pouch and pull down the swing arm of your trebuchet. As you do this you will see that the counterweight is lifted high into the air, (or drops off, if you haven't attached it securely. Keeping your finger firmly on the end of the swing arm, smoothly slide the strings and pouch to the opposite end of your chute. You are now ready launch your missile.

**22** Count down from ten to zero – this is essential to build an atmosphere of tension, excitement and expectation. Then, with a cry of, 'Take this you pesky medieval rat-bags!' or something like that, take your finger off the swing arm and marvel as your missile arcs across the room (or splats you between the eyes).

# START YOUR OWN COUNTRY

This an exciting project involving flags, spies, national anthems, parades, law-making, border controls, hamster licenses, dodgy deals, festivals of culture, fibs and a myriad of other things associated with declaring your independence from Great Britain, Leicester, Tibet ... or wherever else you happen to live.

**NB: These are just 'suggestions' for what you might like to do when you start your own country. You and your dad can probably come up with lots more fun and entertaining ideas.**

## WHAT TO DO

• Think of a name for your country. Anything you like really, for instance: 'Ernie Wets The Bed', 'Fluffy', 'Aubergine Parthenon', 'Olly-Olly Nib Nab', The People's Republic of Custard', 'Mine's A Spaniel', 'Nitwit Zydeco' ... the possibilities are endless.

● Design a really impressive flag for your new country. It could be based on something you're very fond of, for example, a snazzy little number featuring an attractive 'chicken nugget' motif or 'playful kittens' theme. Alternatively, go for one of the fashionable 'designer splodges' favoured by multinational companies.

● Choose a ruler. This could be you or your dad. For instance you could be Prime Minister with your dad as Minister of

Defence (or Minister of de 'fence', if he happens to mending it). However, don't fall out over who gets to be top banana or you may find yourselves involved in a nasty civil war before your fledgling nation is even up and running.

• Decide on a 'territory' to be your new country. This could be your bedroom, your house and garden, or even your entire street. However, the latter would involve you and your dad either…

a) Persuading all the people in your street to become members of your new 'state' by promising them free Caribbean holidays, live-in butlers, sports cars and weekly visits to health spas … none of which will happen, of course … or

b) Invading every other house in the road, 'conquering' the families who live in them and making kneel before you, swearing an oath of loyalty whilst kissing your 'playful kittens'/'chicken nuggets'/'splodge' national flag.

● Design some new money with a picture of your face on all the coins and notes. Every time your subjects get hold this money, which of course, will make them feel really good, they'll associate their happiness with you and love you all the more.

● Start taxing your citizens 50 per cent of their total income. Also tax them for 'privileges' such as owning hamsters, wearing slippers, walking upright, using mobile phones and 'breathing'. This will make you very rich, very quickly. Set up a secret Swiss bank account to keep your money in.

● Get your country recognized by the United Nations. To do this you must arrange to meet 'Mr Ban Ki-moon' in the United States of America at a busy railway station and hand him £5,000,000 dollars in plain brown envelope whilst winking at him like a one-eyed owl on steroids. Ban Ki-moon is the Secretary-General of the United Nations.

● Set your public relations machine in motion by getting your 'PR' staff to circulate favourable images of you to TV stations and newspapers, featuring you doing all the 'modest and unassuming stuff' which makes up your everyday life such as 'bravely diving into swamps filled with crocodiles to save some drowning orphans', 'singlehandedly creating fabulous 5-star banquets for your hordes of adoring celebrity pals', 'captivating thousands of your ecstatic fans with your genius-level singing and guitar playing' and 'scoring goal after goal for your new country at the World Cup'.

● Make some new laws. For instance, 'Backwards Tuesdays', on which everyone must use the name 'Ted' at least three times in every sentence, wear their underpants on their head and walk backwards. Also make it law for everyone to have a picture of you in every room in their house.

● Invent a totally false external threat to your new country such as an imminent invasion by Ghengis Khan, the Visigoths or Julius Caesar. Then, when you aren't invaded, your citizens will love you for saving them from the enemy hordes.

● Introduce a new national sport or pastime such as horse wrestling or 'worms and ladders' (played with live worms) whilst banning all other sports and pastimes. Then introduce a horse tax and a worm tax.

- Set up border controls where, if people don't pay you huge amounts of money to enter or leave your country, sniffer dogs will stick their noses in their luggage.

- Write 'a recently discovered history' of your new country making sure that all your rellies and ancestors are picked out as having played pivotal and crucial roles in all its most important moments including the invention of fire, the wheel, the steam engine, television, antibiotics, dental floss and self-winding garden hoses, as well as having played heroic and decisive parts in building of the Pyramids, the founding of the Roman Empire, the Battle of Trafalgar, the Blitz and the 1966 World Cup Final.

# IP DIP DIP! AN UNDERWATER SAFARI! GO POND DIPPING

Pond dipping is brilliant fun and, now that so many people are taking a new interest in nature, it's once more becoming really popular. When you swash your net around in a natural pond, you really are taking a 'lucky dip' in an underwater environment which is wriggling with masses of fascinating creatures, including monstrous great diving beetles, cute caddis fly larvae, barmy backswimmers and ferocious dragonfly larvae. There's no telling what you might come up with!

But, before you set off with your buckets, jars and nets here are some...

## IMPORTANT HEALTH AND SAFETY NOTES!

**1** It's quite easy for an over enthusiastic pond dipper to not only hurl their jar into the pond, but themselves too! So always take your dad with you to fish you out if you do happen to throw yourself in. Your dad may also have gone pond dipping as a lad, so he might be able to offer you some dip-tips.

**2** Kneel at the water's edge as you pond dip and, if you're in a group of dippers (collectively known as a 'despondence'), don't run or push.

**3** Don't get pond water in your mouth. It could have harmful bacteria in it (and, more to the point, if you accidentally swallow some tadpoles, you'll end up with a belly full of frogs\*).

**4** Make sure you wash your hands after pond dipping, especially before eating.

\***This might not be true.**

## WHAT YOU NEED ↘

● A NET: Any sort will do but the best kind are the professional ones sold by nature and science suppliers who, as you'd expect, are listed on the inter ... net! You can also buy nets from fishing-tackle shops or pet-fish shops (but not fish and chip shops).

● SUITABLE CLOTHING AND FOOTWEAR: Don't wear your best ballet shoes and party frock for pond dipping, as it's often a quite messy pastime. You're probably going to be standing in mud, so wear wellies and also take waterproofs with you in case it rains.

● CONTAINERS: You can buy professional pond-dipping trays for examining your catch and keeping it in, but a light-coloured washing-up bowl or ice-cream container is almost as good. White is the best colour because you can see your wrigglers and squigglers really easily.

● IT'S BEST TO HAVE TWO SORTS OF CONTAINERS: big ones for your main catch and smaller ones for looking at the individual creatures more carefully as you try to identify them. Plastic cutlery containers are especially good for separating your species.

● SMALL, WHITE PLASTIC SPOONS AND TEA STRAINERS: Use these to a) scoop out your little wrigglers and get a really close look at them b) transfer them between containers.

● A GOOD QUALITY MAGNIFYING GLASS: This will enable you to behold your captives in all their gorgeous glory.

● IDENTIFICATION SHEETS, BOOKS AND NATURE SPOTTERS' GUIDES: To identify what you have caught.

- **PENCIL AND PAPER:** To make notes and do drawings of your catches.
- **CAMERA:** For taking photographs of the 'prisoners'.

## WHAT TO DO

**1** Find a pond, canal or stream, preferably one that's teeming with all sorts of wildlife (rather than teeming with abandoned supermarket trolleys and empty crisp packets). Your local nature club or wildlife trust might be able to tell you a good place to go pond dipping. Alternatively, you can join one of the organized group pond-dipping expeditions that are advertised on the Internet.

**2** Half fill your containers with pond water and put them on the ground about two metres away from the pond.

**3** Gently sweep your net in a figure-of-eight pattern in the water for about 15 seconds.

**4** Smoothly raise your net from the water and carry it to your large container.

**5** Turn the net inside out in the water so that your catch tumbles into it (or races back to the pond).

*TIP: IF SOME EXTRA-STROPPY LITTLE SQUIGGLERS ARE RELUCTANT TO LEAVE THE NET, SWISH IT AROUND UNDER THE WATER FOR A WHILE.*

**6** If you've been lucky, you will now discover that your containers are teeming with all sorts of wriggly, twitchy little creatures including water fleas, tadpoles, great diving beetles, water snails, pond skaters (and tiny striped dolphins). But if it isn't, don't give up, just dip again.

**Important note:** Treat the little creatures you've caught gently and respectfully. They're very delicate and sensitive, so definitely don't shout at them, call them names or laugh at their unusual appearance. (Well, they can't help being so totally weird, can they?) And use your plastic spoon or tea strainer to pick them up, not your fingers!

**7** Find out about the life cycles of your mini-critters and discover where they fit into nature's 'food chains'.

**8** If you're intending to take your water creatures home so that you can study them a bit more, leave your little captives in plenty of water somewhere cool and shady.

**9** If you're not intending to take your catch home, gently tip the little creatures back into the pond.

*TIP: DON'T LEAVE THE BIG 'PONDOPOLIS' PREDATORS SUCH AS DRAGON FLY LARVAE AND GREAT DIVING BEETLES IN THE SAME CONTAINERS AS YOUR OTHER POND CREATURES OR YOU MAY RETURN TO FIND THEY'VE EATEN THEM ALL (AND POSSIBLY THE PLASTIC CONTAINER, TOO).*

**Important note:** Do not attempt to stuff your pond creatures then mount them on your bedroom wall as 'trophies'. Not only is this considered to be environmentally inappropriate, but it is also ... dead naff!

Finally, something to remember: If you're planning on dipping several ponds make sure you sterilize your pond-dipping equipment between dips. That way if a pond has some horrid lurgy in it you won't transfer it from pond to pond.

# BUILD A FIRE OUT OF DOORS

At one time everyone had at least one 'open' wood or coal fire in their house but nowadays most people keep warm with gas fires and central heating which are very convenient, but rather boring. Open fires are magical, cheerful things which are not only great for cooking, getting warm, creating light (and keeping wolves at bay) but are also really beautiful, constantly changing shape and colour as they hiss, roar and crackle. But of course, fire is also a very, very dangerous thing, so making one involves taking lots and lots of care and thinking twice about everything you do. The sort of fire you're going to build is the kind which human beings have been creating for thousands of years ever since the days when hairy, monkey-like creatures crouched in caves slobbering, gnawing the flesh from mammoth bones (and checking their lottery tickets).

## WHAT YOU NEED ↘

- A knife
- A fire flash, or 'metal match' as it's sometimes called
- Some normal matches
- Some stories (to tell around your campfire)
- An axe
- Bucket of water (And a direct line to your local fire station)

**WHAT TO DO**

**Choose a spot to build your open-air fire.** You must keep your fireplace well away from highly inflammable things such as fields full of crops, dry bracken, tents, overhanging tree branches (dynamite factories and swimming pools full of aviation fuel).

**Prepare your fireplace:** Clear all the stones, leaves, twigs, (dead werewolves), and other debris from a circle about one metre in diameter to prevent your fire from spreading. Doing this will enable you to create a 'no-burn' zone which will also protect any little creatures hidden in the leaf litter which would otherwise be roasted alive (what do you mean, 'Hmm, tasty!'?).

**TIP:** IF YOU'RE BUILDING YOUR FIRE IN THE SNOW, LAY SOME GREEN LOGS SIDE-BY-SIDE TO MAKE A DRY PLATFORM FOR IT.

Now build a low semi-circular wall of logs or stones around part of your fireplace to reflect the heat towards the spot where you're going to be sitting.

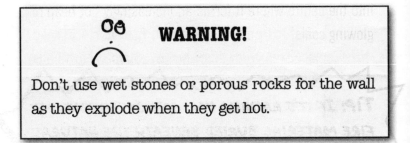

## WARNING!

Don't use wet stones or porous rocks for the wall as they explode when they get hot.

**Collect your fire materials.** You start a fire with tinder. This includes things like birch bark, dead pine needles and straw. Next collect your kindling. This is the stuff you put on the fire once the tinder is lit, and it includes things like dried pine cones, twigs, dead leaves and dry rotted wood. The final thing you have to gather is your fuel, that's the stuff that will create the real heat. If you're going to keep your fire going for a long time you'll need a lot of this. It can include stuff like dead branches, logs, and even dried cow poo.

**Lay your fire.** Make a teepee shape with your kindling. There are other ways to lay a fire, but we won't go into them now (as it will definitely cause your brain to go into 'meltdown'). Even wet wood will burn on teepee-shaped fires once they really get going. All you do is continue to add to the teepee shape while the burning wood collapses into the centre where it forms an increasingly hot heap of glowing coals.

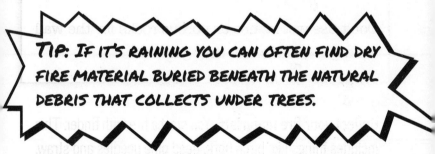

**TIP: IF IT'S RAINING YOU CAN OFTEN FIND DRY FIRE MATERIAL BURIED BENEATH THE NATURAL DEBRIS THAT COLLECTS UNDER TREES.**

**Light your fire.** The easiest way to do this is to strike a match and touch the flame to your tinder. However, if it's raining heavily and your matches are wet, you will have to use your fire flash. Or, you could just pretend it's raining and use the fire flash anyway. Holding the tip of your fire flash on your tinder, rub down on it with the end of your knife blade so that sparks jump from the metal to the tinder. Once the sparks cause the tinder to glow, blow on it until a flame appears then transfer it to the centre of your kindling teepee. Keep building the teepee with your kindling until you've got a really good blaze going. Now you can begin to add the main fuel, still keeping the teepee shape and increasing the thickness of the wood you add (but stop at entire oak trees).

Unless the idea of having no eyebrows, seeing your shoes melt on your feet and going completely bald in a 'flash' appeals to you, never get too close to your fire. Also remember that fires are extra dangerous on windy days. A spark can be blown over a considerable distance then land on inflammable material, creating an uncontrollable inferno. And bear in mind that an unexpected change in the wind direction can cause flames to be suddenly be licking hungrily at your beloved velvet loon pants or best ball gown as your lungs fill up with acrid choking smoke and your eyes smart like they're being stung by giant hornets.

**IMPORTANT SAFETY ADVICE**

**DO NOT SKIP THIS BIT!**

**NEVER LEAVE YOUR FIRE UNATTENDED.** While you're off looking for more fuel it may well get out of control and, before you know it, the entire forest could be on fire. Or, it might simply go out (the fire, not the forest). So make sure that all of your fuel is gathered in advance.

Finally, when you're finished with your fire, make sure it's entirely out before you leave it and that the site looks just as it did when you found it. To do this, tip water on the fire until it's completely out.

# THE HOLE TRUTH – PLAY A GAME OF MINIATURE GOLF

**WHAT TO DO**

**1** Go to a miniature golf course and pay the miniature golf attendant your entry fee.

HAVE YOU GOT ANYTHING SMALLER?

ATTENDANT

**2** You will now be given a) a coloured ball – each player gets a different colour ball so that they don't get them mixed up (because, unlike 'proper' golfers, miniature golfers are mostly considered to be really stupid) b) a putter c) a score card. Player number 1 keeps score for player number 3, number 3 for number 2 and number 2 for number 1 (unless number 3 is rubbish at sums, in which case you should choose your friends more carefully).

**3** Just like big people's golf, there are 18 holes on most miniature golf courses. The idea is to get around the course hitting the ball the least number of times. Quite irritatingly, you also have to get the ball to drop in all the holes.

**4** If you are player number 1, place your ball on the little spot in front of hole 1. Now take hold of your putter.

**WRONG**      **RIGHT**

If you are right-handed, hold the grip of your putter with your left hand above your right hand. And the other way round if you're left-handed. Or either hand if you're ambidextrous, whatever that means.

**5** Now, stand quite close to your ball with your knees slightly bent and your body curled over it. Remember: your feet should be about a shoulders' width apart (that's your shoulders, not Arnold Schwarzenegger's).

WRONG          RIGHT

**6** Hold the 'blade' of your putter next to the ball, swing it back and hit it (preferably in the direction of the hole). When you hit the ball, make sure that all of your body below your hips remains completely still. However, this should not be the case when moving between holes. Also keep your head completely still when you're hitting the ball. And remember! The bigger your swing, the further your ball will go.

**TIP: VISUALIZE AN IMAGINARY LINE GOING FROM THE BALL TO THE HOLE AND WHEN YOU HIT THE BALL TRY TO MAKE IT FOLLOW THAT IMAGINARY LINE.**

**7** When everyone has hit their shot, the person whose ball is furthest from the hole gets the next hit (because you all feel so desperately sorry for them). Then it's the turn of the next furthest and so on.

**8** Each hole on the course has a 'par'. This is the average number of hits it should take an average player to get their ball in the hole (and is intended to make new players cry by making them realize they're completely rubbish at miniature golf).

**9** As you progress around the course you will come across all sorts of 'hazards' which are designed to make the game more challenging and exciting (or just plain annoying). For instance, some holes are around a corner. In which case you will have to make your ball rebound off a wall (or your opponent's head).

**10** When the last ball has been holed, add up how many hits each person has taken altogether. The person with the least number of hits is declared the winner.

## SOME THINGS YOU MIGHT LIKE TO DO TO GIVE YOURSELF AN ADVANTAGE DURING PLAY

a) Arrive at the miniature golf course with a glove hanging out of your back pocket. This is what real golfers do, and the sight of a really well turned-out glove may well terrify your opponents.

b) Arrive at the golf course with a 'caddy'. This is someone who carries a massive bag containing your clubs and advises you on technique and club choice for each shot. As miniature golf actually only involves one club, the presence of a caddy is totally unnecessary, but will definitely give you a psychological advantage.

c) When your opponents are just about to hit the ball either i) make a low rumbling sound in your throat ii) quack like a duck … or iii) begin whistling tunelessly.

d) If your opponent hits a bad shot, offer them your sympathy then start sniggering behind your hand ... or simply jeer them mercilessly.

e) As your opponent is about to take a crucial shot which could mean winning or losing the game, start patting your head whilst rubbing your stomach in a circular motion.

f) If you've hit a rubbish shot, suddenly point skywards and cry, "Look at the size of that!" whilst stealthily moving your ball with your foot so that it's in a much better position for your shot.

g) Conversely, if your opponent's hit a really good shot, suddenly point skywards and cry, "Look at the size of that!" whilst moving their ball with your foot so that it's in a much worse position for their shot. When asked, "Look at the size of what?" just reply, "The sky. Isn't it awesome?"

# GROW SOME THUMPING GREAT PUMPKINS

Pumpkins are brilliant fun. They're great to look after and to watch as they grow from a tiny seed the size of a grain of rice to massive plants with fruits the size of beach balls. Then, when you've harvested them, you can carve them into all sorts of amazing shapes and designs and light them up or simply use them as missiles in totally barmy pumpkin-chucking competitions.

## WHAT YOU'LL NEED ↓

● Some pumpkin seeds. There are at least 30 different sorts of pumpkins ranging from smallish Baby Bears to medium-sized Jack o' Lanterns and absolutely whopping Atlantic Giants, which are the variety you should choose if you want to grow really stonking great mega-pumpkins the size of Bristol.

● A garden or some big grow bags or big tubs.

● Some plastic pots, measuring about 10 cm across the top diameter.

● Some seed compost.

## WHAT TO DO ↘

**1** In early April put some seed compost in your plastic pots, leaving about 2.5 cm of space at the top.

**2** Put a single seed in each pot edgeways on so that water doesn't lay on it and make it rot.

**3** Cover it in a thin layer of seed compost then water it gently.

**4** Put the pots on a seed tray without holes and leave a shallow covering of water on the bottom so that the pumpkin plants can have a good slurp whenever they feel thirsty.

**5** Keep your pumpkin pots somewhere warm and light such as a south-facing windowsill (or Tunisia). Never let them dry out.

**Very important:** Please resist the temptation to dig up your pumpkin seed to see how it's doing. This will make it very unhappy! So, as the doctor said to the shrinking man, "You'll just have to be a little patient!"

**6** After about two weeks you'll see a real miracle taking place as the pumpkins' leaf-like 'dicotyledons' push up through the compost followed by their stalks. Congratulations, your seeds have germinated into little pumpkin plants.

**7** You should soon see true leaves beginning to appear. These leaves will now begin to photosynthesize. In other words, they'll start taking carbon dioxide from the air then using the energy from the sun and the green chlorophyl in their leaves to convert it into the sugars that pumpkin plants find so yummy. Meanwhile, underground, the pumpkin plant is pushing lots of roots out to take nutrients from the compost (greedy, aren't they?).

**8** You should now move your rapidly growing plants to a greenhouse or cold frame. But if you've not got either of them don't worry. But if you do move them and there's a chance of frost, bring them back indoors (then get in bed with them).

**9** If you see the pumpkins' roots coming through the holes in the bottom of their pots, gently transfer the plants to bigger pots.

**10** It's now time to plant out your pumpkins. You should do this at the end of May as it's unlikely that there'll be any more hard frosts then. First dig a hole about 60 cm x 60 cm x 60 cm. Fill it with well-rotted cow manure (having first found a well-rotted cow) then add a bit of fish, blood and bone fertilizer, which you can get from all garden centres.

Alternatively, fill your grow bags or tubs with a mixture of compost, cow muck and fish, blood and bone fertilizer.

**11** You now need to get your pumpkin plant out of its pot without damaging it and with as much of its 'root ball' remaining attached to it as you possibly can. This can be quite tricky as its roots will have wrapped themselves around the inside of the pot and will be quite reluctant to part company with it. The best way to release them is to first add water to the pot then 'tease' the roots (by telling them they're wimps or insulting their nodules). No, not really, you actually 'tease' by gently pulling at the compost-covered roots until they slowly untangle themselves and come free from the pot.

**12** Now gently place your pumpkin plant in the hole you've made so that the soil surface is level with the bottom of its stem, firm the soil around the stem by pressing your hands on it, then water it well.

**13** Leave spaces of around 2 metres between your pumpkin plants, as they'll need plenty of room for sending out their very long tendrils.

**14** As your pumpkin plants grow, you must water them and feed them regularly with stuff like liquid feed or chicken muck pellets (but definitely resist the temptation to offer them crisps, cheeseburgers or choccy biscuits). One way to make a liquid feed is to stir cow muck into a plastic rubbish bin full of water, strain the resulting 'cow's bum gravy' (as top horticulturalists refer to it) through a sieve into a bucket then slop it around the base of your pumpkin plant.

**15** You must also talk* to your pumpkin plants telling them to drink their 'cows bum gravy' or they won't grow up big and strong like Jack's bean stalk.
*optional

**16** As the summer progresses you'll see big yellow flowers appearing on the pumpkin plants. Hopefully, you'll also see bees flitting from flower to flower as they pollinate the female flowers with pollen from the male ones. Not long after this you'll see baby green or yellow pumpkin fruits forming behind the female flowers. Hurrah!

**17** Now your pumpkins will begin swelling rapidly. If you want just a single massive pumpkin, 'nip out' all the other fruits leaving only one so that it gets all the nutrients to itself and grows to the size of the Taj Mahal.

**18** You may now wish to gently lift your pumpkins off the wet soil and put straw under them so that their bottoms don't get dirty, but this isn't absolutely necessary.

**19** At the end of the summer you'll see the wonderful sight of your pumpkins slowly turning a gorgeous burned orange colour (or into coaches pulled by white mice). When they're a deep, vibrant orange colour it's time to harvest them. Use a sharp knife to cut them and remember to leave plenty of stalk on them so they'll keep longer.

So that's it, you've grown some magnificent thumping great pumpkins!

# WE'LL CROSS THAT ONE WHEN WE COME TO IT – BUILD A BRIDGE ACROSS A STREAM

## WHAT YOU NEED ↘

- A stream
- Some logs and sticks
- Some clay and mud
- Some small stones and sand
- A shovel

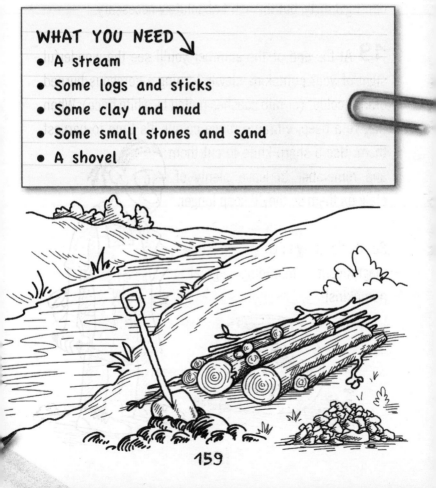

**WHAT TO DO**

**1** Choose a narrow and shallow, 'friendly' sort of stream to build your first bridge across. In this way, if your bridge does happen to collapse, you will only get wet feet, rather than being swept out to sea and eaten by big stinky things with eyes on stalks. Of course, as you become more confident with your bridge building, you may wish tackle more challenging water obstacles e.g. the Avon Gorge, the Mississippi River, the English Channel.

**2** Find 2 strong logs that are about the same length. Make sure the 'diameter to length ratio' is about one to twelve.

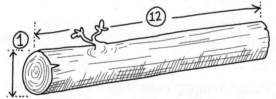

**3** Test the strength of your logs by hurling them at the ground (making savage grunting noises and slobbering copiously). If they crack or break they're rubbish for bridge building – so find two more.

**4** Lay your logs across the stream about 60 cm apart whilst making sure:

a) that they're level b) that there's at least 30 cm of log resting on both banks and c) that they don't wobble.

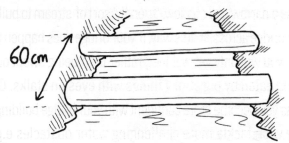

60 cm

**5** Optional: If you want your bridge to last for yonks and not be destroyed by floods, aircraft carriers or rampaging great white sharks, you'll need to 'raise' it by resting each log-end on a rock, or another log. Again, make sure they don't wobble.

**6** Lay lots of those thick, brown, 'sticky' things, otherwise known as sticks, across your logs, making sure they're strong enough to support your weight. If you can't find sticks that are long enough, move your logs closer together.

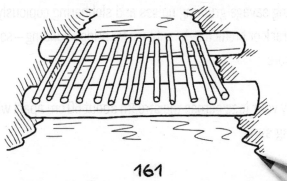

**7** When all these 'cross sticks' are in place, shovel about 5 cm of thick mud on top of them, smoothing it out so that it's level and firm. If the mud drops through any gaps between the sticks, fill the spaces with smaller sticks.

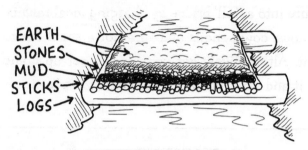

EARTH
STONES
MUD
STICKS
LOGS

**NB: Do not be tempted to lick your fingers when carrying out this part of the activity.**

**8** Spread a thin layer of small stones on top of the mud then shovel about 5 cm of fairly dry soil on top of the stones.

**9** Now take off your shoes and socks and slowly walk backwards and forwards across the bridge packing the soil solid with your feet.

**10** Add another 5 cm of soil then pack that down in the same way.

# CONGRATULATIONS!
Your bridge is now finished.

**SUGGESTION:** Why not turn your fabulous new structure into a 'toll' bridge by charging local rabbits, hedgehogs, cows, snails and whatnot a small fee to cross it. Alternatively get your dad to set up home under it and wait for three billy goats to appear.

---

## WARNING.    θθ
︵

Use your bridge with care. Unlike a dog, a bridge is not for life. It will quickly deteriorate as the logs go rotten, and rain, frost and wind damage it. Even stonking-great bridges made from bolts the size of wrestlers' thighs, cast iron girders like tree trunks and the sweat of big smelly men fall down. In December 1879 the humungous Scottish Tay Bridge collapsed taking an entire trainload of passengers with it!

---

# LEARN HOW TO WHIP A TABLECLOTH OUT FROM UNDER A LOAD OF DISHES WITHOUT BREAKING THEM (HAVE YOU GOT WHAT IT TAKES TO 'PULL IT OFF'?)

## HOW IT WORKS (MORE OR LESS)

We perform tasks better if we understand the principle behind them. In other words, if we know how they work. So here's a brief explanation of how the tablecloth trick works.

After a tablecloth and a dish of his mother's apple pie (or something like that) fell out of a tree and landed on the head of the mega-famous scientist, Sir Isaac Newton (1643–1727), he dreamed up all sorts of stuff to do with gravity and motion and not-motion, or 'inertia' (as slackers like to call it). One of these things was something he named the 'first law of motion' in which he states that an object will stay completely still i.e. inert, unless something bashes into it. So, applying this law to the tablecloth trick, your task is quite simply to keep the impact of the moving tablecloth on the dishes to a minimum. You should also learn to pull your tablecloth really quickly, as the less time that the tablecloth is rubbing against the dishes, the less chance it has to set them wobbling.

Or, as Sir Isaac would have put it:

MORE DASH
+ LESS BASH
= LESS CRASH

A quick word about science friction: You must also be aware of 'frictional' forces when performing this trick. If you try it with a thick or textured table cloth or, even worse, one made of freshly cut yak wool, there is far less chance of it succeeding than if you do it with a nice smooth and thin, untextured cloth which will, of course, lessen the amount of frictional force on the dishes.

And finally: resist the temptation to glue the objects to the tablecloth to stop them falling over ... that's just pathetic.

## WHAT YOU NEED ↓

• A rectangular table with a really smooth top and sharp edges i.e. unrounded

• A soft, smooth and seamless, rectangular tablecloth with no stitched 'hems'

• At least 25,000 dishes. No, not really, just some plastic dishes to practice with then some pot dishes for the real thing.

## WHAT TO DO ⟶ ↓

**1** First iron your tablecloth really well to make sure that it's superbly smooth and totally free of wrinkles (unlike your dad).

**2** Carefully lay the tablecloth on the table so that it's completely flat and crease-free.

**3** Arrange your tablecloth so that the edge of the end furthest away from you is perfectly in line with that far edge of the table. However, at the end which you're going to be pulling from, there should be enough cloth overhanging the table edge for you get a good grip on it.

**4** Arrange your dishes on the table. The first one should sit in the exact centre. Use plastic dishes to start with. Weigh them down with some fruit or something similarly heavy, as this will make them more 'inert', but don't fill them with hot soup or beef curry.

**5** Stand in the exact middle of the edge of the tablecloth that you'll be pulling and grasp it with both hands.

READY?

CAT

167

**7** Now start 'bunching up' the overhanging tablecloth with both hands. Keep 'bunching' until you reach the edge of the table.

**8** In one smooth and seamless movement, 'yank' the tablecloth downwards, niftily stepping back from the table as you do.

**Important note:** Whatever you do, don't pull the tablecloth outward or upward or the dishes will come with it.

**9** Once you've got the hang of pulling the cloth out from under plastic dishes replace them with breakable ones and perform the trick in front of an audience.

**10** Now either...
a) sweep up all the broken dishes from the floor ... or
b) bow to your delighted audience as the sound of their rapturous applause fills your ears.

## OR TRY THIS...

If you can't be bothered with the cloth and dishes rigmarole (or don't have any tablecloths or dishes in your house), try this alternative trick. The principle's just the same.

**1** Place a sheet of paper on the edge of a table with about 10 cm hanging off the edge.

**2** Put some coins on it.

**3** Lick your finger and quickly strike the hanging paper with a downward motion. This should slide the paper out from under the coins without the coins moving.

**4** Now try the trick with coins in stacks or standing on their edges.

# CREATE AN AWESOME 'TARZAN'-STYLE ASSAULT COURSE IN YOUR GARDEN

Men and woman who want to join super-tough military units like the commandos have to complete a challenging and exhausting assault course involving things like whizzing down death-defying zip-wires, wading up to their necks in mud and clambering over enormous barriers.

Using a bit of imagination and the sort of stuff you find lying around in your shed, garage, or local DIY store, it's possible to make your own 'Tarzan'-style assault course. Then, once it's complete, you and your pals can test your skill, stamina and courage whilst finding out who can get around the course the fastest.

**IMPORTANT SAFETY NOTE** Even though it's nowhere near as hazardous as the real thing, the obstacles in this DIY assault course can still be very dangerous if they aren't put together carefully and securely. Get your dad to carry out rigorous safety checks before anyone attempts the assault course.

## WHO YOU NEED ↓

• A 'sergeant major' to rant mercilessly at the 'commandos' as they stumble, slip and stagger around the course while he yells, 'Get on wiv it, you 'orrible little child!' and stuff like that, i.e. your dad (who is, no doubt, like this anyway).

• Someone to time each commando as they complete the course. This also could be your dad.

• A judge to make sure no one cheats or skips obstacles. Your dad might enjoy doing this.

• A starter. Ideally this should be someone like err ... your dad!

## THE OBSTACLES

Here are some ideas for obstacles on the course. However, they don't necessarily have to be set up in this order.

**1** A tunnel to crawl through: Get some thin bendy plastic plumbing piping and cut it into lengths – the size depends on the height you want your tunnel to be. Stick the ends of the pipes in the ground at intervals so that you end up with a series of arches. Drape a plastic 'tarpaulin' over the arches to make your tunnel. Weight the edges with soil or stones. A simpler but less challenging tunnel can be made from tables or chairs.

**2** Balance beam: Balance a plank on two boxes. The narrower the plank, the harder the challenge. Set it above a paddling pool filled with water (piranhas and alligators).

**3** Stepping stones: This could be a series of mats, pieces of cardboard, carpet or anything else which will lie flat. Place them far enough apart for the 'commandos' to have to leap from one to the next, increasing the distance with each gap. Anyone who falls off has to start this obstacle again.

**4** Rope swing across a 'swamp'. Your swamp can be anything from a hole full of mud to paddling pool filled with water. Or even just an imaginary swamp marked out with string. Of course you will need something sturdy to tie your rope to such as a tree branch.

**5** Car tyres obstacle. Spread the tyres along the assault course so that the 'commandos' have to put one foot inside one, then the other foot inside the next, as they progress along the route.

**6** Ladder obstacle: Lean a ladder against a strong table or small wall at 45 degrees. Climb the ladder then jump down the other side. Important: make sure the ladder is fixed securely so that it does slip when you're on it.

**7** Hurdles/'limbo dancing' poles: this is series of broom handles or canes laid across chairs. Alternate jumping over them and 'limbo dancing' under them.

**NB: if you use canes, put something on the sharp ends or wrap them in gaffa tape so that they aren't dangerous.**

**8** A ramp: This can be as simple as a plank or large piece of strong wood leaning against something sturdy such as a wall. Again, it must be fixed securely. Run up the ramp and jump down the other side.

**9** Water obstacle: Fill a paddling pool with water (or warm custard) so that the competitors have to splash through it to reach the next obstacle.

**10** A section of the course where you must hop, skip or even have your legs in a sack to complete the entire length.

# CREATE SOME 'CUTTING EDGE' PLANT SCULPTURES – THEY'RE A SNIP

People have been cutting and training bushes and shrubs to grow into weird and wonderful shapes for centuries. They've made the geometric shapes called parterres, amazing mazes and labyrinths to get lost in, knot gardens where hedges are clipped to give the impression they've actually been tied in knots and all sorts of awesome 'shrub sculptures' ranging from full-size elephants to aeroplanes and ogres. And during the 1960s, at Disneyland U.S.A., someone had the idea of clipping shrubs into Disney cartoon characters, which increased shrub-sculpting's popularity even more.

The art of clipping and training shrubs into elegant, intricate, unusual and amusing shapes is known as topiary and, with a bit of patience and effort, anyone can do it. It's tons of fun and after some careful clipping, it's possible end up with a permanent Diplodocus, Dalek or Great Dane in your garden which will be a constant source of admiration and amusement for visitors and passers-by (and terror and confusion to small dogs and short-sighted people).

> EXCUSE ME, COULD YOU DIRECT ME TO THE NEAREST GARDEN CENTRE, PLEASE

So, don't beat about your bush! Get clipping!

**WHAT YOU NEED** ↘

• Topiary shears, hedgecutters, secateurs or even just a pair of scissors will do for doing your cutting and clipping. Whatever cutting tools you choose, make sure they're really sharp, otherwise they may 'bruise' the plant you're trimming rather than do clean snips.

# ALL OPTIONAL ↘

- Masking tape
- Chicken wire
- Wire frames
- Bamboo canes for guiding

- **SOME PLANTS.** The best sort for clipping into snazzy shapes are evergreen shrubs and trees which have lots of little leaves that grow close together. Evergreens keep their leaves all year round (the clue's in the name), so you don't have the disappointment of seeing your brilliant works-of-art go completely bald in the autumn. Some of the most popular topiary plants are box, yew, privet, holly and lonicera and they can be bought at most garden centres.

- **A BIT OF PATIENCE:** Topiary is a sort of 'slow-motion sculpture'. In other words, it's the sort of thing you have to work on for a while then leave alone so it can grow on a bit before you go back to it. Once your topiary specimen has begun 'filling-out' into the shape you're aiming at, you go back to it and snip again to get that clean and crisp top topiary effect.

Of course, if you don't want to be bothered with the clipping and training bit you can also buy ready-cut topiary shapes from garden centres. However, they'll cost you an absolute fortune, at least ten times the price of the same shrub in its unclipped state! And think of the satisfaction you get from knowing you've created this work of art with your own clever hands. Not to mention the profit you could make if you decided to sell your living sculptures!

## WHEN TO DO IT

With topiary, you have to remember that you're working on a living thing and that living thing has times it would far rather be left alone than have some idiot with shears snipping away at its most treasured bits and bobs when they're at their most tender stage. So, whatever you do, don't start snipping at your target topiary plant in March because that's when its shoots will very delicate and most easily bruised, or even killed, especially as their raw clipped ends are vulnerable to frost. It's much better to do your snipping from June onwards when the new growth is strong enough to put up with a little 'haircut'.

## WHAT TO DO

**1** Get inspired by looking at topiary in books and on the Internet or visiting amazing topiary gardens of which Britain has dozens! This website has a section where you can search for topiary gardens: www.britainsfinest. co.uk/gardens.

**2** Decide upon the shape you wish to create: ball, box, racing car, bird, spiral, cat, seat, lollipop, battleship, Dalek (or small scruffy bush). Actually, it's probably best to start off small and simple. The easiest shapes to begin with are balls, pyramids and cubes. And there's no need to shape a really big shrub. If you do start out with something small and simple, you'll be more likely to have the satisfaction of a successful first project rather than experiencing the frustration of having snipped off more than you can sweep up.

**3** Decide what type of plant you would like sculpt and whether it's going to live in the ground or a pot. Of course, if you start off with a potted plant, you can always transfer it to the garden when it outgrows the pot. It's easiest to start your topiary with a small young shrub that can be trained as it grows. However, if you and your dad are feeling really confident and adventurous, you could tackle a larger, 'grown-up' plant in your garden.

**4** To clip a small cone, ball or cube shape you can either begin by shaping it 'by eye' or you can create a clipping guide by making a frame of your chosen shape with chicken wire, tape or bamboo canes.

**5** Let the natural form of the shrub inspire or suggest the shape you're going to clip.

**6** Work slowly and steadily. Remember, what you're doing to start off with is 'training' your hand to feel its way around the shrub.

**7** Don't rush it and remember to keep standing back from your masterpiece-in-the-making to make sure things are 'shaping up' just the way you want them to.

**8** Once you've successfully clipped a ball, cone or cube shape, you may feel more adventurous and want create a spiral shape. You can do this by winding masking tape around a cone-shaped shrub and using that as your guideline for clipping.

**9** As you become more skilled and adept with your clippers you'll gain the confidence to move onto bigger, more challenging projects such as peacocks, cats or even garden seats!

# LOOK AFTER YOUR TOPIARY

It's important to occasionally remind yourself that your topiary specimen is not a real gorilla or real racing car and therefore, rather than feeding it bananas or engine oil, you must water it and nourish it with plant food to keep it vigorous, happy and healthy.

If your topiary kitten or wizard is in a plant pot, make sure its pot is big enough to allow its roots to expand. Also ensure that the pot is heavy enough to stop it being blown over in high winds.

You should also give your topiary specimen a trim once or twice a year to in order to keep it 'in shape', or even more often than that if it's a fast-growing plant. This is best done in June, remembering that you're aiming to maintain your model's crisp, sharp outline.

# DESIGN AND BUILD YOUR OWN MINIATURE GOLF COURSE

You and your dad, or your mates and their dads as well (or even their dads' dads) could build a miniature golf course in your garden or school playground. It doesn't cost much and you'll get tons of fun from doing the building and playing miniature golf. The key to creating a really ace course is to use your imagination and ingenuity! You'll be amazed at the variety and originality of holes you can improvise with the simplest of materials. And don't forget, you don't have to go the whole 18 holes. Nine, or even six, will do!

**WHAT YOU NEED**
- Materials
- Bricks
- Breezeblocks
- Wooden blocks
- Planks
- Strips of wood

- A bucket
- Cardboard boxes
- Garden stakes
- Flexible plastic plumbing pipe
- Strips of old carpet
- Empty plastic plant pots
- A roll of chicken wire
- Duct tape

TOOLS
- A saw
- A hammer
- Scissors
- Nails ... and a really big bulldozer*
*optional

**WHAT TO DO**

**1** Check out the place where you're going to build your course. Measure its dimensions.

**2** Decide whether you're going to…

a) Use the surfaces that are already there e.g. grass, cement, paving blocks, hard-packed sand etc for your 'fairways'. or…

b) Create 'fairways' out of strips of old carpet or, more expensively, artificial turf (or, even more expensively, diamond-encrusted silk). But remember, the surface mustn't be too smooth or your golf balls will go skidding all over the place.

**3** Decide how many holes there will be and what sort of obstacles you want to include. For instance: mazes, tunnels, ramps, bottlenecks, pools of water (burning forests or concealed pits full of alligators). Don't forget to vary the type of shot needed for each hole e.g. long and straight, curving, uphill (head-over-heels) etc.

**4** Now sketch out a plan of your course including the approximate lengths of each hole.

**5** Using a tape measure, string and sticks, 'plot' where your holes will be on the ground.

**6** Lay down your putting surfaces using the materials mentioned in step 2 remembering to vary the length of your holes.

**7** Edge your fairways with bricks, breezeblocks or strips of wood so that the balls stay on the course.

**8** Mark a 'tee' for each hole, i.e. the spot where you hit the ball from. This can simply be a spray-painted line.

**9** Create the hole by sinking a plant pot in the ground. If you don't want to make actual holes just put the plant pots on their sides and sticky tape them down.

**10** Get creative with your obstacles and hazards. For instance you can create a tunnel with a length of plastic pipe, a ramp with a plank and a breezeblock, a maze with breezeblocks, a water hazard with a sunken bowl of water, a sand trap with hole full of sand, just use your imagination. If you want to get really creative you could make a tunnel at the top of a ramp, a 'mousetrap' from a cardboard box with two entrance holes cut in it but only one exit hole, or a 'forest' using tent pegs.

# MAKE A FACE-MASK COPY OF YOUR OWN FACE (OR ANYONE'S FACE FOR THAT MATTER!)

When someone popped their clogs in the old days their rellies often had a copy of their loved one's mush made so that they could remember what old 'what's-his-face' looked like in years to come. For instance, masks were made from the faces of Tutankhamun, Oliver Cromwell and Napoleon Bonaparte. In many cases these masks were then used to make three-dimensional portraits of the deceased (or wacky fancy-dress party masks). However, once photography arrived there was no longer any need to do this. Nevertheless, not only is making an exact copy of your own face, or anyone else's face, good fun, but it's also a really satisfying artistic project.

**Fascinating fact:** in the 1880s a beautiful, unidentified, young woman was found drowned in the River Seine in Paris. A mortuary worker was so taken with her good looks that he made a plaster cast of her face. When the first ever heart resuscitation training dummy was made in 1960, its face was based on this mask.

## IMPORTANT SAFETY WARNING BEFORE YOU BEGIN!

If your model complains of irritation or burning when you place the gauze strips on their face, remove them immediately. They may be having an allergic reaction.

## WHAT YOU NEED ↘

- A face – your own/your dad's/your mum's/your gran's ... (you choose). Definitely DO NOT choose anyone under 10 years of age. Your model must not smile, open their eyes or move their face for about 20 minutes. They must also remain calm for the whole time.

- A shower cap
- A sun lounger or long table
- Old newspapers
- Vaseline
- Drinking straws cut into 8-cm lengths
- A bowl of warm water
- Scissors
- A roll of plaster gauze
- Some old clothes
- A towel
- A mask
- Some paper towels

A quick note about plaster gauze: Plaster gauze, or sculpting gauze as it's also called, is gauze with dried plaster powder in it. When you dip it in water the plaster is activated giving you time to 'model' shapes with it before it dries hard.

**WHAT TO DO**

- Cut your plaster gauze into strips about 4 cm wide and 10 cm long. Also have some strips cut into triangle shapes and smaller sizes for the awkward bits of your model's face. Have at least 20–30 strips ready to dip. Cover your entire working area, including the floor, with old newspaper.

- Get your victim – sorry, your model, to wash and dry their face. Now ask them to lie back on the sun lounger or table, wearing old clothes and with their head resting on the rolled-up towel.

- Put the shower cap on them to protect their hair then gently smear their face with the Vaseline to protect their skin from the plaster gauze. Be especially sure to coat their eyebrows with Vaseline, but be careful not to get it in their eyes.

- Put a piece of plastic straw up each of your model's nostrils (they usually have two of these).

- Ask your model to close their eyes. Holding a strip at each end, dip it in the warm water for a few seconds. Squeeze the excess water from it and apply it to your model's face, plaster side up. Now soak a second strip and repeat the process. Important: Don't soak more than one strip at a time or they'll become unworkable too soon.

- Start at the edges of the face, overlapping the strips as you work. Remember that you'll be leaving the eyes and mouth until last. You should end up with a mask that is two strips thick. Don't forget to follow the contours of the face and to smooth down the gauze with wet fingers as you work. Take care not to cover the nostrils and mouth opening or your model will suffocate to death!

Remember: After four minutes the plaster will start to harden and the gauze will become unworkable. It will take about 15 minutes for the gauze to dry properly so during this time keep your model calm and entertained, perhaps by playing them some soothing music – but on no account tickle them or tell them jokes!

When the gauze is almost dry, it's time to remove the mask from your model's 'fizzog'. Do this by getting them to gently move their jaw from side to side and open and close their mouth in order to loosen the face mold. Now carefully lift the mold from their face. Take care not to squeeze or pull it as it still needs more drying time and is quite easy to crush or break if you're clumsy with it. Also take care not to pull off your model's nose, lips or eyebrows as you're removing the mold.

# BUILD AN OUTDOOR WOOD-BURNING PIZZA OVEN

This is a big, exciting project that family, friends and neighbours will love both you and your dad for. Food, such as pork, roast vegetables, bread and pizza, tastes about a hundred times better if it's been cooked in a clay oven. You'll already know this if you've been to a restaurant with a clay oven and enjoyed the pizza with its tasty charred base and delicious wood-smoke flavour. Clay ovens are great to keep warm around on chilly summer evenings and also look really good in your garden.

## WHAT YOU'LL NEED
### THE MATERIALS
- Builders' sand
- Clay
- Water

196

- 12 wooden beams each measuring
100 cm x 20 cm x 20 cm*
- 12 90-degree iron brackets and screws
- Wood chips
- Old newspapers
- Rubble
- Bricks

* We're building our oven base from wood but if you and your dad are dab hands at bricklaying you might wish to make it from bricks.

**THE KIT**

- A wheelbarrow
- A tarpaulin or thick plastic sheet
- A big knife
- A shovel
- A drill
- A spirit level
- A bucket
- A saw
- A trowel

## WHAT TO DO

**1** Decide where you're going to build your oven. For the base you'll need a space about 120 cm x 120 cm with room around it to stand while you're working.

**2** Build the base. Get the ground clear and level then build the base walls by placing the wooden beams on top of each other and overlapping them like this. Use

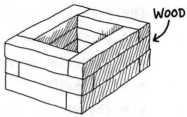

WOOD

your spirit level to ensure the timber is level and fix it in place by screwing a bracket inside each corner at each level.

**3** Fill the middle of your base with rubble to a level about 40 cm below the top then finish it off with a layer of sand, remembering to leave space for the brick floor of your oven.

**4** Lay the bricks in the remaining space and brush sand into the spaces between them.

**5** Build a sand dome-shaped 'former' on top of the bricks. This is simply a temporary 'shaped' pile of sand that will provide a base for your clay dome. It should be about 40 cm high with a diameter of 80 cm. When

CLAY NEWSPAPER

you're happy with its shape, firm it with your hands then cover it with a layer of wet newspaper.

TIP: STAND ON THE BASE WALLS TO LOOK DOWN AND CHECK OUT THAT YOUR FORMER IS PROPERLY DOME-SHAPED.

**6** Puddle your clay. To do this you tip two buckets of sand onto your tarpaulin/thick plastic sheet then take one bucket of clay and throw little lumps of it onto the sand then stamp and twist your feet on the clay until they mix together. Once the bucket of clay is gone you should have the right 2:1 mix.

TIP: YOU COULD GET LOTS OF OTHER PEOPLE TO HELP YOU WITH THE PUDDLING - PUT ON YOUR WELLIES AND SOME SOUTH AFRICAN 'GUM BOOT MUSIC' THEN STAMP AND TWIST THE NIGHT AWAY.

**7** Build your clay dome. Make a long rounded brick shape with a dollop of your mixture then 'mold' it onto the base of your sand dome taking care not to move the sand. Keep adding 'bricks' until you have a ring of them around the base, then begin the next layer. Keep going until the whole dome is covered with a smooth layer of clay. NB Remember to keep the bricks the same thickness. Leave it to dry for at least 4 hours.

**8** Draw a semicircular hole on the front of your oven big enough to fit your pizzas and roasts through. Now carefully cut this out with your large sharp knife then slowly and carefully remove the sand dome from inside the oven.

**9** Fire your oven. Build a little fire in the doorway of your oven then once it's burning use a metal rake to push it back into the oven space. Keep adding more wood and pushing the fire until it's in the centre-back of the space.

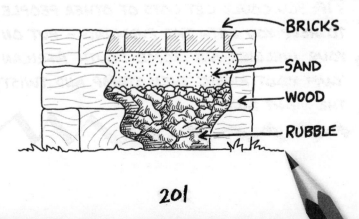

BRICKS

SAND

WOOD

RUBBLE

201

**10** Make the brick arch over the entrance by making a semi-circular sand 'former' then building bricks up over it and using your sand-clay mix to hold them in place. The last brick you place should be the 'keystone' at the top. When it's dry carefully remove the sand.

**11** Make the chimney. Draw a circle just behind the brick arch then drill holes around it so that you can safely remove the solid clay. Build a 20-cm-high chimney around the hole using more puddled clay and also use the puddled clay to fill any gaps between the arch entrance and the chimney.

**12** Mix some unpuddled clay with water to create a sloshy 'soup' then mix it up with a wheelbarrow full of wood shavings. Now make 'bricks' like you did before to create the insulation layer i.e. the bit that keeps the heat in. Leave it to dry.

**13** And finally, add one more layer of puddled clay using the brick technique.

Your oven is finished. Now cook something in it.

# TAKE PART IN THE MOST DRAMATIC MOMENTS IN HISTORY! THE NEXT BEST THING TO A TIME MACHINE

'The Battle of Hastings, the assassination of Julius Caesar, Custer's Last Stand, the burial of Tutankhamun, a Medieval jousting tournament ... yes, I was there! And at lots, lots more amazing events in history.'

Imagine being able to say that! Well, of course, until a time machine's invented, you can't. But you can do the next best thing. And that's get involved in a historical reenactment, or a 'living history' event, as they're also known. They take place all over the world, with thousands of people becoming a completely different person from their normal day-to-day selves, immersing themselves in times gone by, perhaps living the life of a medieval peasant, Apache Indian or Tudor child at the court of Henry VIII, or maybe thrilling to the roar of cannon, the smell of cordite and the sight of charging infantry at the English Civil War Battle of Bosworth.

If you're mad on history, love acting, showing off and dressing up, enjoy the great outdoors and want to carry on thrilling to the sort of imaginative play that's been giving you a real buzz since you were knee high to a chariot wheel, then historical reenacting is definitely the thing for you!

You can reenact five minutes of history, five hours or five days. And it won't necessarily involve spending lots of time and money on costumes and equipment. But it can if you want it to! The main thing is to use your imagination. You can be scriptwriter, director, historical researcher, costumier, actor and producer all at once. And learn loads of scintillating historical stuff while you're doing it. You can do reenactments in your own back garden or join a big reenactment society and take part in huge historical events such as the Battle of Waterloo or the Viking invasion of Britain. Brilliant!

**WHAT TO DO**

**1** Go and watch a living history event and get inspired.

**2.** Now choose a favourite place and time in history. Decide upon a particularly exciting event during that time. Find out as many details as you can about the event and who was involved. Lose yourself in the historical time you've chosen by reading fiction and non-fiction books about it, watching movies set in that period, reading on-the-spot accounts written by people who lived then and doing your own internet research.

**2.** Decide who you're going to be. Once you've chosen your character, find out everything you can about your new 'persona': how they dressed, what they ate and drank, how they talked, what made them happy, what made them sad, what they believed in, who their friends and family were.

**3** Get your teachers, friends and friends' dads (or even their dads' dads' dads) involved in your project, inspiring them with your own enthusiasm and exciting, action-packed accounts of events in history, so that they're desperate to become their own favourite characters in the sort of scenarios which really rattle their cutlasses and stir their porridge! And then it will be up to you to orchestrate whatever scenario you've chosen to revive, whether it's going to last three minutes or three hours!

Or … find a historical reenactment group and join it, taking part in whichever slice of living history is their particular passion. They'll no doubt welcome you and your dad and will probably set you up with costumes and equipment until you get round to providing your own.

However, if you are thinking of dashing around the battlefield at Waterloo and ferociously clashing swords with Napoleon's grenadiers, you may have to wait a bit, as most groups don't let children do really dangerous stuff until they're 12 or 13. And people do occasionally get hurt when they're caught up in the excitement of reenacting.

But don't despair, there are masses of other exciting roles for you to act out such as a knight's page, lady-in-waiting, camp follower, groom, goose-girl, street urchin, child crusader or pickpocket (and who knows, you may already be one of these characters in real life). There are reenactment groups for just about every period in history. For instance, there's a lost Roman 9th Legion group;

Gladiator Schools groups; War of the Roses groups; Wild West groups with screaming Apache Indians, blazing six-shooters and beleaguered wagon trains! And nearly all of these groups have a website with tons of exciting info plus photographs of their amazing events.

SORRY ABOUT THAT. LUCKY WE'RE ONLY PRETENDING!

**4** Once you take part in your first event and become your 'other self' from the past you'll realize why living history is all so exciting. Possibly even discovering your hidden acting skills as you show off before the crowds who come in their thousands to watch living history events. Or it might be the smell of gunpowder and saddle leather that you thrill to, the sight of galloping cavalry and the sound of braying bugles. Or your satisfaction might simply come from the huge relief you feel when you flop down in your cosy centrally heated home and enjoy dinner in front of the telly after enduring days of wind and rain in a freezing cold tent in itchy clothes and really uncomfortable shoes whilst surviving on gristle, grits and gruel.

So, what are you waiting for? Go pretend! And you never know, you may end up getting the opportunity to take part in a blockbuster movie battle or crowd scene. Film producers frequently go to living history groups when they're looking for 'extras'.

# DIG THIS! SET OFF IN SEARCH OF BURIED TREASURE

Imagine how the four French boys must have felt when they found the awesome prehistoric cave paintings at Lascaux, all by accident! Or how Howard Carter felt when he first entered the tomb of Tutankhamun and set eyes on all that amazing treasure which had lain undiscovered for thousands of years. Now think of all the stuff that's in your house. Or maybe your shed and garage. Then think of all the things that millions of other people have in their houses, sheds and garages. Then look at a photo of a Victorian street scene and think about all the stuff in that: the horse-drawn coaches and wagons; top hats and umbrellas; toys and tools; the horses' harnesses; the policeman's truncheon, notebook and whistle; the coins, keys and pens in people's pockets; the bottles, boots, buckets, pans and pots in shop windows ... the list is endless. Now take yourself further back in history and think of all the millions of people who've lived in Britain including the Celts, the Vikings, the

Romans, the Saxons, the Normans, the Tudors (the Teletubbies and the Wombles) and imagine all the stuff they had in their villas, houses, barns, stables, forts, factories, workshops, dairies, prisons, palaces, hovels and all the other places where they lived their lives.

For thousands of years, human beings have been creating things, using them, then losing them, throwing them away or deliberately hiding them. And, although much has been burned or rotted to grot, loads of this stuff is still around. And most of it is under the ground! Yes, we're all walking on top of buried history!

So why not go in search of this hidden loot! All you have to do is get yourself a metal detector and go combing farmers fields (or hair-dos) for lost relics of battles or ancient coins which may have been dropped by long-dead warriors, travellers or farm workers. You can also discover the sites of ancient rubbish tips and dig amongst the detritus of centuries. Or, if you don't want to go too far afield, you can simply dig up a patch of your own garden! And you'll learn tons of fascinating history and geography along the way!

## WHAT YOU NEED ↓

- A METAL DETECTOR: Really posh ones are computerized and lightweight with a screen which indicates the size and density of anything it finds. Some are so sensitive that they are able to discover really tiny coins buried as deep as 22 cm below the surface. You can also get ones specially designed for use by children. But your metal detector doesn't necessarily have to be up-to-the-minute or brand new. A huge Anglo-Saxon treasure trove was discovered using a 14-year-old one.

- HEADPHONES: Some treasure hunters use these to cut out background noise so that they can pick up the slightest change in tone, which might indicate something very special.

- SPARE BATTERIES for your metal detector.

- MAPS: both up-to-date and old plus a compass or sat-nav.

- A SMALL PICK AXE, trowel and hand rake for doing your digging with.

- A MAGNIFYING GLASS for examining your finds.
- TOUGH CLOTHES AND SHOES which will protect you from all that nature can throw at you.
- GARDENERS' STRAP-ON KNEELING PADS to protect your knees when you're on all fours scrabbling around in the dirt.
- WATER AND FOOD: Treasure hunting can be thirsty work and you also need to keep up your energy levels.

## WHAT TO DO

**1** Get inspired … by this brilliant example of what a determined treasure hunter can discover! In 2009, a man with a 14-year-old metal detector was searching a field near his home in Staffordshire when he discovered no less than a mind-boggling 1,500 pieces of buried Anglo-Saxon treasure that had lain untouched for almost 1,300 years! Now that really is a find!

**2** Carry out this research and preparation…
a) Decide the area where you're going to locate your treasure hunt, taking into consideration the sorts of things you're going to be looking for.

TIP: SOME OF THE BEST PLACES FOR FINDING RELICS ARE OLD BATTLEFIELDS, DESERTED MEDIEVAL VILLAGES, LONG-FORGOTTEN RUBBISH DUMPS FROM VICTORIAN AND EDWARDIAN TIMES, GREEN LANES*, CANAL TOW-PATHS, SITES OF OLD WORKSHOPS, HOSPITALS AND FACTORIES. REMEMBER: A LOT OF TREASURE HUNTERS FIND QUITE

AMAZING THINGS IN WHAT AT FIRST APPEAR
TO BE VERY ORDINARY PLACES.
*GREEN LANES ARE THE NETWORK OF
BRIDLEWAYS AND LONG-DISTANCE TRAILS
USED BY PEDDLERS, MERCHANTS AND DROVERS
OF HERDS OF ANIMALS FROM PREHISTORIC
TIMES UNTIL THE ARRIVAL OF MODERN ROADS.

b) Look at old ordnance survey maps. This is an excellent
way to discover the location of long-forgotten fascinating
places where there might have been things such as old
leather-works, potteries, breweries and bakeries. You can
get copies of these from your local county council archives
and records department.

## THINGS YOU MIGHT FIND

**1** Hair pins, clay pipes, kitchenware, buttons, toothbrushes,
toys (ye olde i-poddes) and other everyday objects from
the past.

**2** Remnants of old industries including pottery, bits of

leather and 'hand-blown' ink bottles, beer bottles and medicine bottles.

**3** Weaponry such as gun barrels, musket balls and sword hilts.

**4** Animal bones: Most of them of them will be quite recent. But you never know, you might come across something really awesome such as the hyena skull which was discovered at Creswell Crags in Nottinghamshire. Imagine that?! Finding the skull of an animal that roamed Ice-Age Britain along with woolly mammoths and sabre-tooth tigers.

**5** Fossils such as trilobites and ammonites from millions of years ago.

**4** Old coins, jewellery, ornaments, gold drinking cups, brooches and other historical 'treasures'!

**5** Things that have disappeared more recently; such as modern coins, car keys and rings.

## IMPORTANT THINGS TO REMEMBER WHEN YOU'RE ON THE HUNT!

● Take care! When you're digging for relics you should always be aware that you might come across other, possibly dangerous, things, including gas pipes, electricity cables, water pipes, phone lines, sewage pipes (and hibernating cave bears).

● If you're hunting for interesting objects in a long-abandoned rubbish tip look out for sharp-edged stuff such as jagged or broken glass. Wear tough gloves when you're fossicking in order to protect yourself from sharp objects and dirt.

● If you ever come across anything such as a bomb, bullet, shell or any other lethal object, do not touch it. Get well away from it then contact the police and tell them what you've found.

- If you're exploring abandoned buildings, always do it in the company of your dad and take lots of care! These places can be incredibly dangerous, with holes in their floors, staircases that could give way when you're halfway up them, walls that might collapse on top of you and hundreds of other unseen hazards!

- Remember, to search abandoned buildings you must have written permission from the owner.

- Do not trespass. Before you go on to anyone's land, first seek their permission. Farmers often draw up an agreement with treasure hunters that states what share each of them will get should they find anything of value.

- Respect the Country Code: close gates after you, do not damage crops, frighten animals or disturb nesting birds.

- Leave everything as you found it. If you dig up a buried object, fill in the hole and neatly replace the turf you removed when you began digging.

HAPPY HUNTING!

# NOTES FOR DAD